101
FIRE ZONE BLITZES

LEO HAND

ISBN: 1-58518-699-6
Library of Congress Control Number: 2002107459
Cover design: Jennifer Bokelmann
Diagrams and Layout: Deborah Oldenburg
Front cover photo: Brian Bahr/Allsport

Coaches Choice
PO Box 1828
Monterey, CA 93942
www.coacheschoice.com

DEDICATION

For Mary.

ACKNOWLEDGMENTS

Thanks to my wife, Mary, for urging me to follow my heart and return to big city coaching even though it involved her making sacrifices.

Thanks to Raina for the adjustments she had to make.

Thanks to Tony Shaw for giving me the opportunity to coach in Texas.

Thanks to Jim Murphy, Don Kloppenberg, and Will Shaw for all they taught me about defense at Long Beach City College.

Thanks to the wonderful people of the Zuni and Navajo Nations who taught me much more than I taught them during the seven years I lived with them.

Thanks to Joe Griffin for giving me one of the best coaching jobs in California.

Thanks to all of the splendid young men whom I have been privileged to coach.

Thanks to all of the great coaches whom I have been fortunate to have worked with and coached against.

Thanks to Phil Johnson for all of his help and kind words.

Thanks to Conrado Ronquillo, Joe Barba, and the maintenance crew at Irvin High School for all of their patience, kindness and help during this project.

Thanks to Sam Snoddy for his assistance during this project.

Thanks to the offspring whose ancestors endured the Middle Chamber and the Long Walk for all of the contributions that they have made to the greatest game of all.

Thanks to Howard Wells for giving me the chance to coach at El Paso High School.

Thanks to Knifewing, whose music helped inspire the words of this book.

Thanks to Herman Masin, editor of Scholastic Coach, for all of his help and suggestions during the past 30 years.

Thanks to Dr. James A. Peterson for all of his help and encouragement.

CONTENTS

CHAPTER 1

FOOTBALL'S NEWEST DEFENSIVE STRATEGY:

HOW THE FIRE ZONE BLITZ WILL HELP YOU WIN GAMES

The fire zone blitz is one of the most innovative and exciting defensive strategies to ever arrive on the football scene. The following four factors illustrate how this new strategy can help any coach win games:

FACTOR #1:   It limits the number of receivers an offensive opponent can put into a pass pattern and safely protect its quarterback by holding the offense accountable for blocking all of the defenders in the box. This goal is accomplished by a tactic called *illusion*. At the snap of the ball, as many as seven or eight defenders will attack the line of scrimmage and give the offense the *illusion* of a *total blitz*. Once the defense reads pass, however, only five pre-determined defenders will continue to rush the quarterback. The remaining *fake blitzers* will drop off into coverage. To compound the offensive problem even further, the *fake blitzers* may be defensive linemen. The offense, therefore, never knows (until it is too late) which defenders will rush the quarterback. In the old days, the defenders who lined up in three-point stances were pass rushers, and the players who lined up in two-point stances were either pass rushers (if they blitzed) or coverage players. Today, every player aligned in the box is both a potential pass rusher and a coverage player. The fire zone blitz has, therefore, rewritten the rules of pass protection by creating a chaotic guessing game for the offense.

FACTOR #2: The fire zone blitz has the potential to eliminate *double-read pass protection* schemes and force offensive linemen to frequently end up *blocking air*.

FACTOR #3: A fire zone scheme has the potential to either eliminate a quarterback's hot read or force him to quickly dump a short pass off to a hot read in a long-passing situation.

FACTOR #4: The fire zone blitz is also deadly versus the run because the seven or eight defenders aligned in the box are attacking and penetrating the line of scrimmage and forcing ballcarriers out of their intended course. As this is happening, at least one secondary defender is reading the ball and backing these defenders up. The fire zone blitz empowers a defense by enabling it to attack an offense rather than having it react to the offense. If in future years, offensive teams try to counter the fire zone blitz by employing formations that feature no running backs, they will become one dimensional, and whenever an offense become one dimensional, it becomes easier to defend.

WHAT'S IN THIS BOOK FOR YOU

This book provides the reader with the following:

- 101 fire zone blitzes from the four most commonly used defenses in football today: the 3-4, the 4-3, the split-4, and the Bear 46.

- All of the techniques and assignments necessary to implement these blitz schemes versus any two-back offensive formation. The scope of this book will not include the adaptation of fire zone blitz schemes to aceback and empty formations. Although it is possible to adapt many fire zone blitz schemes to these formations, assignments and techniques frequently begin to change as a defensive front begins reducing itself in order to make the adjustments necessary to remain sound versus all of the various spread-out aceback and empty formations it may encounter. Through this process, a high degree of *simplicity* is often lost. Having diagramed hundreds of fire zone blitz schemes versus every conceivable aceback and empty formation, it is the opinion of this author that it is a mistake for a coach (especially at the high school level) to try to adapt every fire zone blitz to every possible offensive formation. Most coaches will find it more workable to have their players check to one or two fire zone schemes versus aceback and empty formations.

- An entire chapter on the techniques of blitzing.

- An entire chapter on the defensive secondary skills necessary to implement an explosive zone blitz package.

- Six additional stunt tactics that will greatly enhance the effectiveness of one's fire zone blitz package.

- A fire zone blitz philosophy of defensive football.

HOW THE FIRE ZONE WORKS VERSUS A TWO-BACK SET

Whenever a fire zone scheme is employed, both cornerbacks will play man, one safety will be free, and three defenders from the box will drop into the three underneath zones (will be referred to in this book as **Abel**, **Baker**, and **Charlie**) and share the joint responsibility of covering the tight end and the two running backs. Figures 1-1a through 1-1d show how we number the receivers and the fire zone assignments versus the

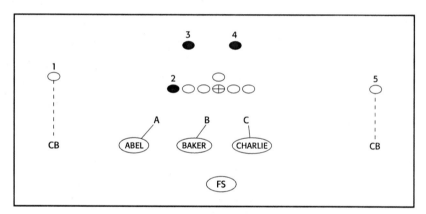

Figure 1-1a

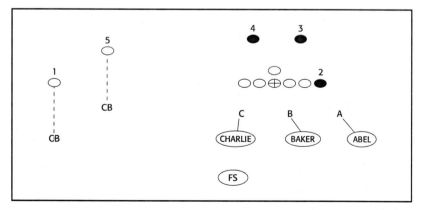

Figure 1-1b

four most commonly used two-back sets. Note the bizarre way in which we number the twins set. We number this set in this manner because we are a corners-over team.

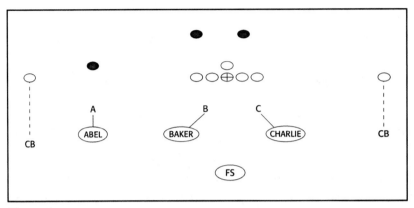

Figure 1c

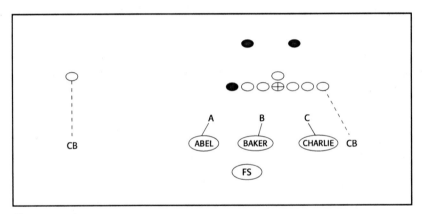

Figure 1-1d

Assignments and Techniques for Abel's Drop:

- Abel drops to a position that will enable him to attain outside leverage on #2.

- Keys #2 to #3.

- If #2 runs a quick out (six yards or less), the defender immediately jumps his pattern and establishes a 3-yard cushion (Figure 1-2).

- If #2 runs a vertical route and #3 runs an out pattern of six yards or less, the defender gains depth and squeezes #2 inside. He should not be in a big hurry to jump #3's out pattern because #2 may turn his vertical route into a deep out. The defender relinquishes his cushion on #2 and tries to work to a depth of 8 to 10 yards. As #3 starts to cross Abel's face, the defender begins to widen and establishes a loose cushion on #3, but tries to stay in the throwing lane between the quarterback and #2 for as long as possible. Baker will help by alerting Abel with an "out-out" call in the event that #2 does turn his vertical route into a deep out (Figure 1-3).

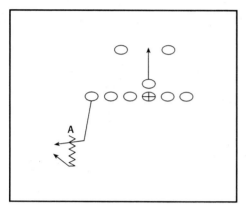

Figure 1-2

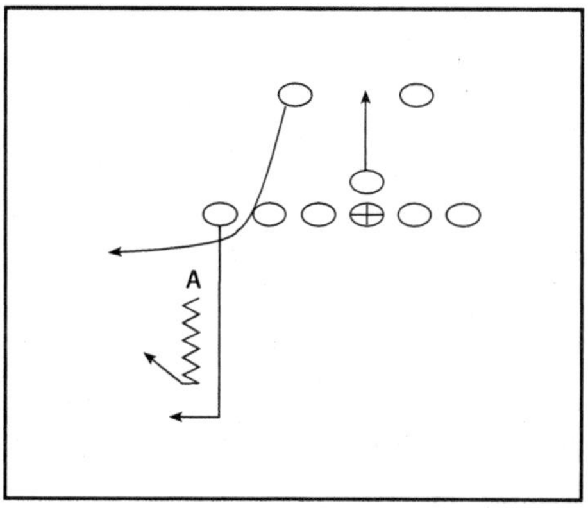

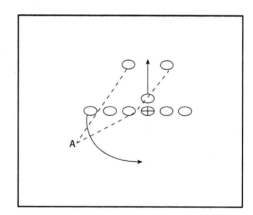

Figure 1-3

- If #2 runs a vertical route and #3 either blocks or runs a short inside route, Abel locks on to #2, squeezes him inside, maintains outside leverage, and forces him to run a collision course (Figure 1-4).

- If #2 runs a quick crossing pattern, the defender keys #3 to #4 (Figure 1-5).

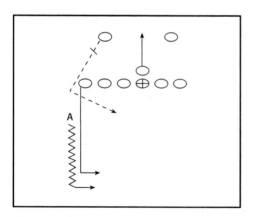

Figure 1-4

Figure 1-5

Assignments and Techniques for Baker's Drop:

- Baker drops to a position that enables him to establish inside leverage on #2, but keeps #3 in his periphery.

- Keys #2 to #3.

- If #2 runs a vertical route, Baker gains depth and covers him from an inside-out position, keeping #3 in his periphery. If #3 blocks or runs a short out pattern, the defender locks on to #2 (Figure 1-6a). If #3 runs a short in pattern, Baker releases his coverage of #2 and locks on to #3 (Figure 1-6b).

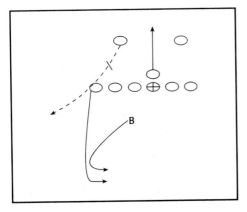

Figure 1-6a

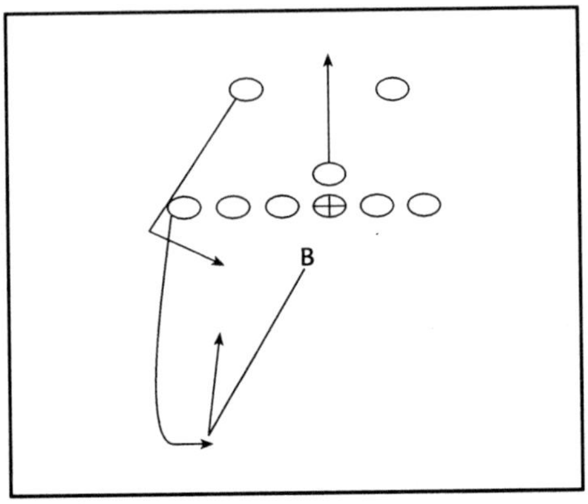

Figure 1-6b

- If #2 runs a quick crossing pattern (six yards or less), Baker immediately calls "in-in," jams #2, walls him off, and forces him to deepen his pattern. The defender then locks on to #2 (Figure 1-7a) unless Charlie echoes Baker's "in-in" call. If Charlie echoes Baker's call, it is because #2 and #4 are crossing. If #2 and #4 cross, Baker releases his coverage of #2, gains depth, and locks on to #4 (Figure 1-7b).

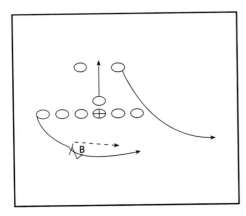

Figure 1-7a

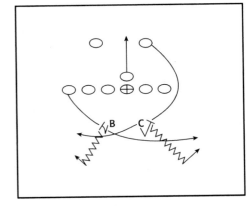

Figure 1-7b

- If #2 runs a quick out pattern, Baker immediately redirects his attention to #3 and covers him (Figure 1-8a). If #3 and #4 try to run short crossing patterns, Baker follows the same rules as when #2 and #4 ran short crossing patterns (Figure 1-8b).

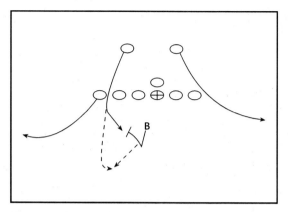

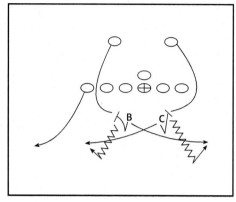

Figure 1-8a   Figure 1-8b

Assignments and Techniques for Charlie's Drop:

- Charlie opens up and drops to a position that enables him to cover #4 from an inside-out position.

- Keys #4, but stays alert for an "in-in" call from Baker.

- If #4 runs a quick crossing pattern (six yards or less), Charlie immediately jams #4, walls him off, and forces him to deepen his pattern. Charlie locks on to #4 (Figure 1-9a) unless Baker has given an "in-in" call (Baker will be the first one to give the call because #2 is aligned on the line of scrimmage and #4 is in the backfield). If Baker calls "in-in," Charlie echoes his call, releases his coverage of #4, gains depth, and locks on to #2 or #3 (Figure 1-9b).

- Charlie covers #4 on all other routes.

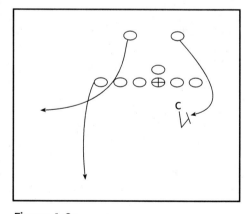

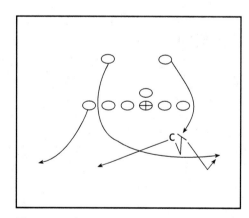

Figure 1-9a   Figure 1-9b

FIRE ZONE COVERAGE VERSUS THE DIRTY DOZEN

Figures 1-10a through 1-10l show how the fire zone would adjust to and cover 12 of the toughest patterns it will ever face.

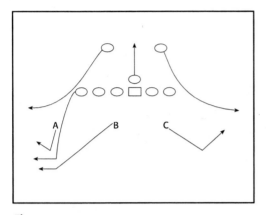

Figure 1-10a

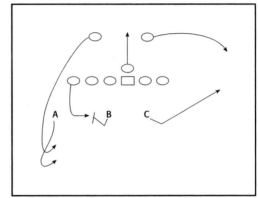

Figure 1-10b

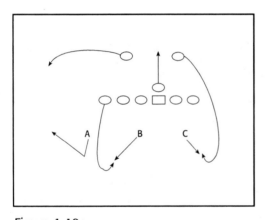

Figure 1-10c

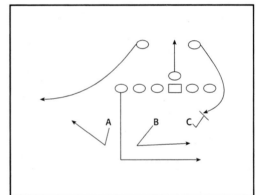

Figure 1-10d

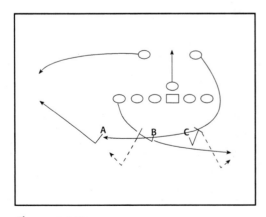

Figure 1-10e

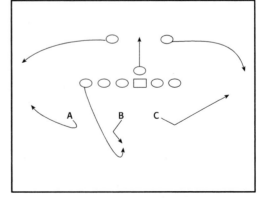

Figure 1-10f

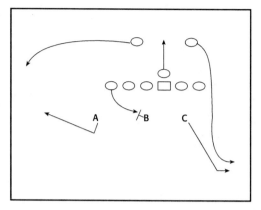

Figure 1-10g

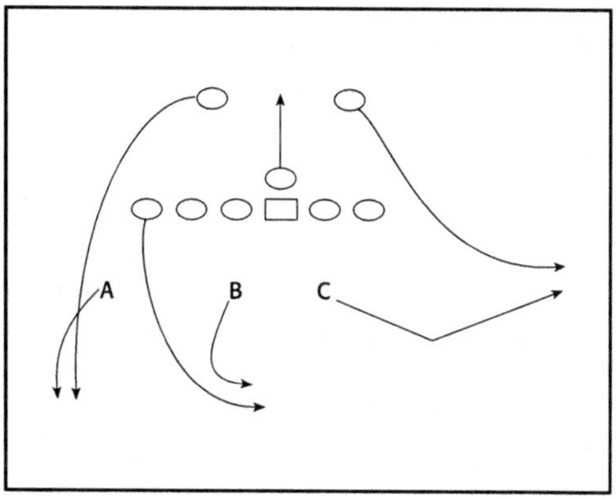

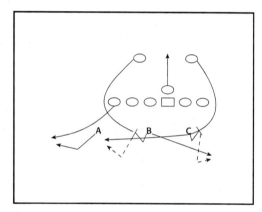

Figure 1-10h

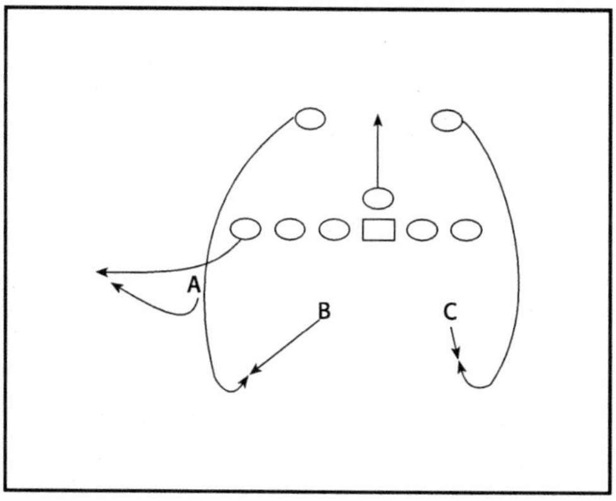

Figure 1-10i

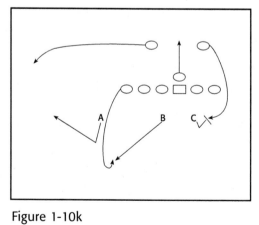

Figure 1-10j

Figure 1-10k

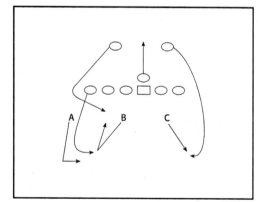

Figure 1-10l

ENHANCING THE FIRE ZONE BLITZ WITH OTHER STUNT TACTICS

The Hybrid Fire Zone

This tactic combines a strongside fire zone concept with a weakside *illusion stunt*. Figure 1-11 shows the strong end and Mike dropping off into coverage and combocovering the tight end and strong halfback (similar to a fire zone Abel-Baker drop). Although four defenders appear to be rushing from the weakside, the weak end is *spying* the weak halfback. This tactic is effective in eliminating double-read pass blocking schemes and forcing offensive linemen to end up *blocking air*.

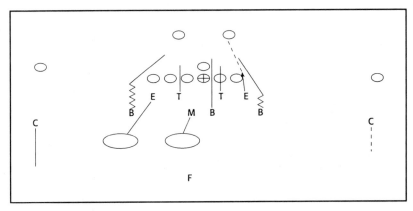

Figure 1-11

The Old School Zone Blitz

Back when Tom Bass was coaching in the NFL, he frequently blitzed linebackers and dropped defensive linemen into coverage. Unlike the fire zone, the pass coverage he used was strictly zone. Figure 1-12 shows a variation of cover 3 sky in which the nose is dropping into coverage.

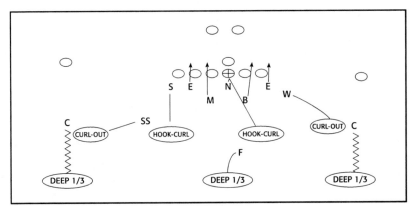

Figure 1-12

Overloads

Overloads attempt to get more pass rushers on one side of the ball than available pass blockers. Figure 1-13 shows a weakside overload that is created by a delayed pass rush by the nose. Every defender on the strongside is employing base reads versus run. Versus pass, Stud and Mike are dropping into coverage, and the nose is rushing through the B gap. The obvious weakness of this tactic is that there is only one strongside rusher, but when used as a change of pace, this stunt will frequently catch the offense off guard.

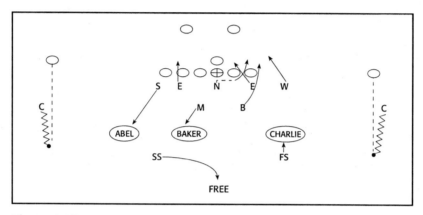

Figure 1-13

Line Twists

Line twists are effective versus man pass-blocking assignments and are easily incorporated into many fire zone blitz schemes. Figure 1-14 shows a delayed line twist involving both ends and both tackles. This twist is a delayed reaction to pass. Versus run, these players will employ base reads.

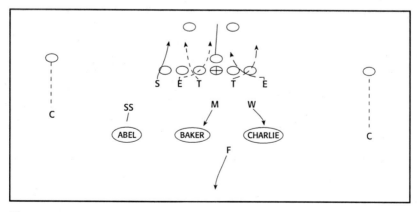

Figure 1-14

Secondary Blitzes

Secondary blitzes and fake secondary blitzes are powerful multifaceted weapons that can be incorporated into many fire zone blitz schemes. Figure 1-15 shows a weakside cornerback blitz.

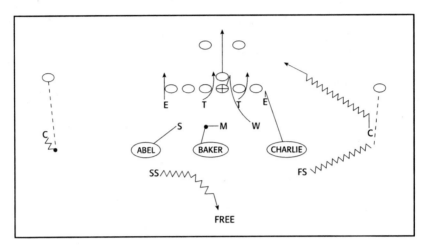

Figure 1-15

Twin Stunts

Whenever two players stunt through the same gap, it is referred to as a *twin stunt*. Figure 1-16 shows both inside linebackers creeping toward the line and blitzing through the B gaps at the snap of the ball. The strong end is also following behind Mike through the B gap. This is an unusual tactic. Since few offensive teams ever see this type of stunt, it is often very effective. Twin stunts are usually called in passing situations.

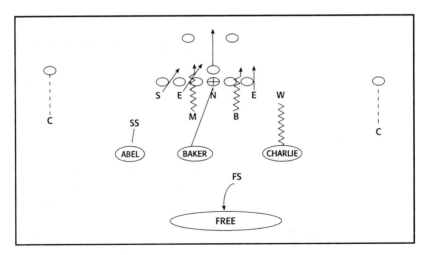

Figure 1-16

CHAPTER 2

BASIC PRINCIPLES
OF BLITZING

- If a player blitzes infrequently, using it as an element of surprise, it's important that he disguises his intention.

- If a player frequently blitzes, disguising his intention may not be as important because he may want to occasionally give the offense a false key by *showing blitz* but then *playing straight* at the snap of the ball. Whichever strategy he decides to use, it is important that he does not establish a pattern that can be exploited.

- A player's eyes are one of his most important tools when blitzing. To be an effective blitzer, a player must be able to see (on the run) the keys that will lead him to the ball. Seeing these keys is the first step in being able to read and react to them.

- Unless the blitz is a delayed reaction to a pass, it is critical that the blitzer is moving, attacking, and penetrating the line of scrimmage at the snap of the ball.

- Blitzers must keep their feet moving at all times. This factor is especially important when they become engaged with a blocker.

- A blitzing player should use his quickness to avoid blockers.

- If the play is a pass, and the blitzer becomes engaged with a blocker, he should keep his hands inside of the blocker's hands and try to maintain separation from the blocker. He should not look at the passer too soon because he may lose sight of the blocker. A blitzer must first defeat the blocker before he can sack the quarterback. While blitzers should have a predetermined pass rush move in mind, they should be ready to change their move according to the circumstance. Blitzers need to take what the blocker gives them and make their move at the appropriate time. Remember that if a blitzing player makes his pass rush move too soon, the blocker will have time to recover. On the other hand, if he makes his move too late, he will probably be too close to the blocker, thereby enabling and the blocker to get into the blitzer's body and nullify his charge. If possible, a blitzer should try to get the blocker turned one way and then make his move in the opposite direction. The blitzing player should also use his forward momentum to manipulate the blocker's momentum. If the blocker's momentum is back, the blitzer should attack him with a power move and knock him backwards. If his momentum is forward, the player can use a move that puts the blocker forward and destroys his balance. Blitzing players should never leave their feet to bat a ball down. They should get their hands up as the quarterback begins his throwing motion, but keep charging toward the quarterback. Too often, when a defender jumps up to bat a pass down, the quarterback will duck under, elude the defender, and scramble out of the pocket.

- If the play is a run, the blitzer should react to his keys and the pressure of blocks as he normally would if he were employing a read technique. Since a blitzer has forward momentum to his advantage, he should use his hands rather than his forearm when attacking a blocker. Blitzing players must maintain separation from blockers and not let them get into their legs. If possible, blitzers should try to make the blocker miss.

- When blitzing, a player should keep his body under control at all times and try to maintain a low center of gravity, and provide as small a target as possible for the blockers.

- Blitzers need to study their opponents' game films carefully. They should know how their potential blockers react and what techniques they favor. It helps to know the strengths and weaknesses of the opponent.

- Blitzers should also study the opponent's eyes as he's getting set at the line of scrimmage. The blocker's eyes will often tell a blitzer where he's going. Studying the pressure that the blocker puts on his down hand when he gets into his stances will frequently give a pass/run or directional key.

- Blitzers who study the scouting report will increase their knowledge of the opponents' formation, down-and-distance, and field-position tendencies. They should use this information to anticipate, but never to guess.

- All players should gang tackle and try to strip the ball out of the ballcarrier's arm.

- Players should never take for granted that a running back or quarterback has been downed. If they arrive at a pile late, they should be on the alert for a loose ball.

- Players must maintain total intensity from the time the ball is snapped until the whistle is blown.

- Before the snap, blitzers should anticipate potential blockers and be prepared to react to those blockers as they penetrate the line.

- On plays directed toward the blitzer's side of the field, he should make the tackle. On plays directed away from that player, he should take the proper angle of pursuit and be in on the tackle. Players should always pursue relentlessly. Remember that if a player is not within five yards of the ball when the whistle blows, he is probably loafing.

- If the backfield action does not indicate flow, a blitzer should protect his gap until he finds the ball. He should never guess.

- If a player is assigned to *spy* (cover a back) when he's blitzing, he should expect that the back will first block and then run a delayed route. Do not allow him to be fooled. Remind him that he must cover the back, no matter what he does, until the whistle blows.

- The ball is the blitzers' trigger. When the ball is snapped, *they're gone*! They should not listen to an opponent's cadence; they're not talking to the blitzer!

Players should not rely upon the lines that are marked on the field. The ball, not the lines, establishes the line of scrimmage.

CHAPTER 3

FIRE ZONE SECONDARY TECHNIQUES

Stance and Alignment

A defensive secondary player should:

- Align himself with an inside shade of the receiver when help from the free safety is not available, approximately seven yards deep.

- Align outside shade of the receiver when help from the free safety is available.

- Set up with a narrow base, feet inside of his armpits, outside foot up (toe-heel relationship).

- Keep his weight on his front foot.

- Keep his knees bent and his hips lowered.

- Slightly round his back with his head and shoulders over his front foot (nose over the toes).

- Allow his arms to hang loose.

- See both the receiver and the quarterback (with his peripheral vision).

Backpedal

A defensive secondary player should:

- Maintain proper leverage (inside or outside) on the receiver. He should not let the receiver get head up with him.

- Keep a good forward lean as he backpedals (chin down and nose over the toes).

- Push off with his front foot and take his first step with his back foot. He should not step forward or lift a foot and set it back down in the same place.

- Keep his weight on the balls of his feet.

- Reach back with each step and pull his weight over his feet.

- Keep his feet close to the ground during the backpedal.

- Not overstride; take small-to-medium steps.

- Keep his arms bent at a 90-degree angle—relaxed, but pumping vigorously.

- Maintain a proper cushion. When the receiver gets 10 yards downfield, the defender should be 15 yards deep. When the receiver is 15 yards downfield, the defender should be 18 yards deep.

- Remember and anticipate that 3-step routes are usually thrown 5 to 7 yards downfield (exception: fade); 5-step patterns are thrown 8 to 15 yards downfield; and 7-step routes are usually thrown 18+ yards downfield.

- Be aware of a receiver's split. Wide splits often indicate inside routes; tight splits often indicate outside routes.

- Keep his shoulders parallel to the line and not let the receiver turn him.

- Mirror the receiver's movements, while keeping his outside shoulder on the receiver's inside shoulder if he's maintaining inside leverage and his inside shoulder on the receiver's outside shoulder if he's maintaining outside leverage.

- Control the speed of his backpedal. When the receiver makes his break, the defender must be under control and able to gather and break quickly in the direction of the break.

- Concentrate on the base of the receiver's numbers until he makes his final break.

- Anticipate a break when the receiver changes his forward lean, begins to chop his feet, or begins to widen his base.

- Honor all inside fakes when he's without free safety help.

- Not backpedal at the snap if aligned on a tight end (versus a double tight set). He must be ready to jump a flat or crossing route.

- Remember that "if the receiver gets even (with him), he's leavin'." Whenever a receiver gets too close, the defender must turn and run with him, keeping his body between the receiver and the ball. He must not allow separation to occur. As he's running with the receiver, he can try to disrupt the receiver's strides by slapping at his near hand and wrist.

Plant and Drive

- When the receiver makes his final break, the defensive back should drop his shoulder in the direction of the receiver's break and explode in that direction. He must make his break parallel to the receiver's break and quickly close the cushion.

- The defender must not lose concentration on the receiver. He should not look for the ball until he's closed his cushion, and he sees the receiver look for the ball.

- If the receiver tries to change direction after the defender has begun his drive, the defensive player should be in a position so that the receiver will have to make contact with him in order to change directions.

Playing the Ball

A defensive secondary player should:

- Attack the ball at its highest point.

- Play the ball, not the receiver when the ball is to his inside and the receiver is outside of him.

- Play the ball through the receiver's upfield shoulder when the receiver is between him and the ball. He should never cut in front of a receiver to make an interception unless he is absolutely sure that he can get two hands on the ball.

- Try to catch the ball or break up a pass with two hands, not one.

- Always knock the ball toward the ground, never up in the air.

- Try to strip the ball if the receiver catches the pass.

- Head to the nearest sideline when he intercepts a pass.

- Always look the ball into his hands and protect it after he catches it.

WHOM CAN THE SAFETY HELP?

Although cover 1 employs a free safety, the two cornerbacks can't realistically count on the free safety to assist them with all deep patterns. The field is simply too wide to expect the free safety to cover the entire area between the two sidelines. Cornerbacks who can expect inside help from the free safety should usually employ an outside-leverage technique. Cornerbacks who can't expect inside help should employ an inside-leverage technique. Figure 3-1 shows three common formation strength/field-position situations that will determine the cornerback's leverage technique.

In Figure 3-1a, the left cornerback cannot expect to receive inside help. He should therefore maintain inside leverage on the flanker. The right cornerback should also employ an inside-leverage technique, because the split end is so close to the sideline. Because both receivers in Figure 3-1b have assumed tight splits, both cornerbacks can expect to receive inside help and should thus maintain outside leverage. Although the ball is in the middle of the field in Figure 3-1c, both the flanker and split end have assumed wide splits. The two cornerbacks should therefore maintain inside leverage, because it is doubtful that the safety can help either of them with inside routes.

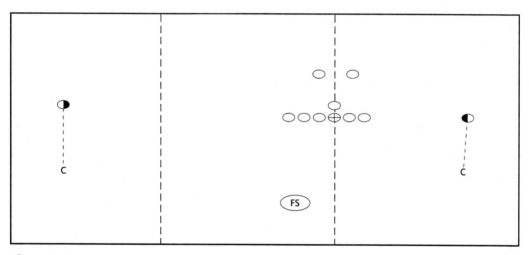

Figure 3-1a

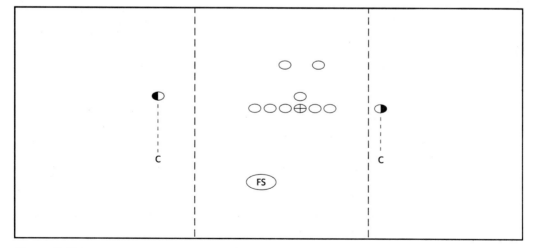

Figure 3-1b

25

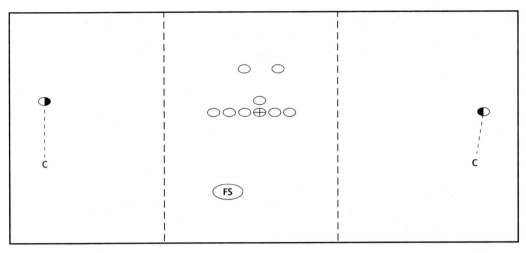

Figure 3-1c

CHAPTER 4

BASE DEFENSIVE TECHNIQUES

Gap responsibilities are lettered as illustrated in Figure 4-1:

Figure 4-1

Technique responsibilities are numbered as illustrated in Figure 4-2:

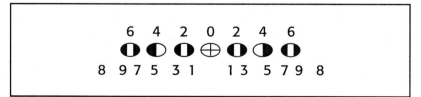

Figure 4-2

0 Technique

The defensive player lines up opposite the center. He is responsible for both A gaps. First, he keys the center and then both guards. He controls the center's block and protects the flow-side A gap. If the guards and center scoop block, he attacks the center and prevents him from blocking a linebacker. If the guard double-teams him, he must not get driven back. Pulling guards usually indicate play direction—he should pursue through the A gap.

1 Technique

The defensive player lines up so that he's shading the inside of the guard. His first step is with his outside foot. He controls the A gap. First, he keys the center and then the guard. The center's head must never be allowed to get across his outside number, and the guard's head must never be allowed to get across his inside number. If the guard pulls across his face, he attacks the center, squeezes the A gap, and watches for cutback. If the guard pulls to the outside and the center tries to reach him, he must avoid or control the center's block and pursue outside. If the guard pulls outside, and the defender feels no pressure, he's being trapped. He should trap the trapper.

2 Technique

The defender plays a 3 technique from a head-up position.

3 Technique

The defender lines up outside shade on the guard. His first step is with his inside foot. He controls the B gap. First, he keys the guard and then the tackle. He controls the guard's block and never allows the guard to hook him. If the guard tries to block inside, and the tackle tries to cut him off, he tries to control the inside shoulder of the guard and keep him off the linebacker. If the guard pulls outside, and the tackle cracks down on the defender, he fights pressure, controls the B gap, and watches for cutback. If the guard pulls outside, and the defender feels no pressure from the tackle, he's being trapped. He should trap the trapper. If the guard pulls inside, and the center blocks the defender, he squeezes the A gap, fights pressure, and watches for cutback. If double-teamed, he must attack the tackle and not get driven back.

4 Technique

The defender plays a 5 technique from a head-up position.

5 Technique

The defender lines up outside shade on the tackle. He steps with his inside foot and controls the C gap. First, he keys the tackle and then the tight end. He must fight the pressure of the tackle's block. If the tackle blocks inside but the defender feels no pressure from the tight end, the play is a trap. He should trap the trapper. If the tackle blocks inside, and the tight end cracks down on the defender, he fights outside pressure and controls the C gap. If he's double-teamed, he attacks the tight end and doesn't get driven back.

6 Technique

The defender plays a 9 technique from a head-up position.

7 Technique

The defender lines up so that he's inside shade of the tight end. He steps with his outside foot and controls the C gap. He must not get driven backwards or crushed inside. If flow goes away, he chases the play as deep as the ball. His visual key is the near back, and his pressure key is the tight end. If the tight end blocks him, and the near back kicks out the defender playing an 8 technique (off-tackle play), he squeezes the play inside out and guards against a cutback. If the tight end blocks him, and the near back shows sweep, the defender should try to work across the tight end's face and pursue inside-out, again watching for the cutback. If the tight end releases, and the near back kicks him out, he squeezes the play inside, keeping his outside foot back. If the tight end releases outside, and the near back shows sprint-out pass, the defender attacks upfield, working across the outside shoulder of the deepest back.

9 Technique

The defender plays outside shade on the tight end. First, he keys the tight end, then the near back, and then a pulling lineman. He steps with his inside foot and doesn't let the tight end hook him in. Versus sweep, he controls the tight end's block, maintains outside leverage, and tries to get upfield and force the ball inside or wide and deep. If the tight end blocks inside, the defender squeezes the C gap and looks for the near back to block him out. If this doesn't happen, he looks for an offensive lineman to trap him. He takes on the blocker and dumps the play inside. He must keep his outside leg free and be prepared for the back to force the play outside. If the tight end releases outside, he first looks to the near back and then to a pulling lineman. He must be prepared to be kicked out, hooked inside, or logged.

8 Technique

This defensive player lines up outside of the tight end. He is responsible for containment. Many variations of this technique exist. Generally, the player playing an 8 technique keys the near back through the tight end. This player may employ a crash technique, a feather technique, or a box technique. He may also line up two yards outside of the tight end, four yards deep, and employ a style similar to a strong safety.

CHAPTER 5

3-4 FIRE ZONE BLITZES

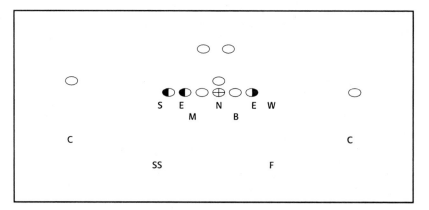

Figure 5-1

Strong cornerback—the cornerback who lines up opposite the flanker.

Weak cornerback—the cornerback who lines up opposite the split end.

Strong safety—the safety who lines up on the tight-end side.

Free safety—the safety who lines up on the split-end side.

Stud—the outside linebacker who lines up in a strongside 9 technique.

Strong end—the defensive end who lines up in a strongside 5 technique.

Mike—the inside linebacker aligned on the strongside.

Nose—the defensive lineman who lines up opposite the center (0 technique).

Buck—the inside linebacker aligned on the weakside.

Weak end—the defensive end who lines up in a weakside 5 technique.

Whip—the outside linebacker who lines up on the weakside.

STUNT #1

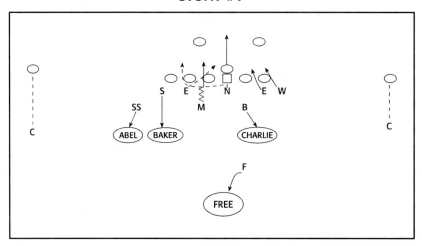

STUNT DESCRIPTION: This **fire zone blitz** features a delayed twin rush by the strongside end and a delayed line twist by the nose.

SECONDARY COVERAGE: Cover 1 disguised as cover 3. The strong safety, Stud, and Buck drop off into coverage.

STRONG SAFETY: Lines up as though he's playing cover 3 sky. Keys the tight end. If he blocks, the strong safety quickly supports strongside run. Drops **Abel** versus dropback pass. Checks the tight end for throw back before pursuing weakside run.

STUD: Plays 9 technique versus run. Drops **Baker** versus pass.

STRONG END: Plays 5 technique versus run. Delay (twin) rushes through the strongside A gap versus pass.

MIKE: Creeps toward the line during cadence. Blitzes hard through the outside shoulder of the guard as the ball is being snapped and secures the B gap.

NOSE: Plays 0 technique versus run. Loops across the face of the offensive tackle and contains the quarterback versus pass.

BUCK: Versus weakside run, scrapes outside and contains. Versus strongside run, pursues the ball from an inside-out position. Drops **Charlie** versus pass.

WEAK END: Slants across the offensive tackle's face into the B gap.

WHIP: Rushes through the outside shoulder of the offensive tackle. Secures the C gap and contains the quarterback.

FREE SAFETY: Free. Plays centerfield. Provides alley support versus run.

STRONG CORNER: Plays cover 1. Inside/outside technique is dependent upon field position and the distance of the flanker's split.

WEAK CORNER: Plays cover 1. Inside/outside technique is dependent upon field position and the distance of the split end's split.

STUNT #2

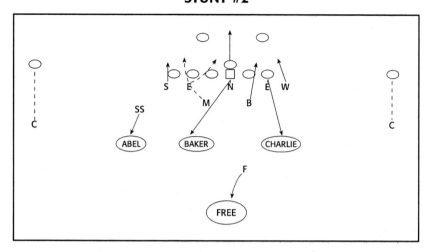

STUNT DESCRIPTION: This **fire zone blitz** features a delayed blitz by Mike.

SECONDARY COVERAGE: Cover 1 disguised as cover 3. The strong safety, nose, and weak end drop off into coverage, and the free safety is free.

STRONG SAFETY: Lines up as though he's playing cover 3. Keys the tight end. If he blocks, the strong safety quickly supports strongside run. Drops **Abel** versus dropback pass. Checks the tight end for throwback before pursuing weakside run.

STUD: Plays 9 technique versus run. Contains rush versus pass.

STRONG END: Plays 5 technique versus run. Slants across the face of the offensive tackle into the B gap versus pass.

MIKE: Plays base technique versus run. Versus pass, delay blitzes through the outside shoulder of the offensive tackle.

NOSE: Plays 0 technique versus run. Drops **Baker** versus pass.

BUCK: Blitzes through the outside shoulder of the offensive guard and secures the B gap.

WEAK END: Plays 5 technique versus run. Drops **Charlie** versus pass.

WHIP: Rushes hard from the outside. Contains the quarterback and weakside runs. Chases strongside runs.

FREE SAFETY: Free. Plays centerfield. Provides alley support versus run.

STRONG CORNER: Plays cover 1. Inside/outside technique is dependent upon field position and the distance of the flanker's split.

WEAK CORNER: Plays cover 1. Inside/outside technique is dependent upon field position and the distance of the split end's split.

STUNT #3

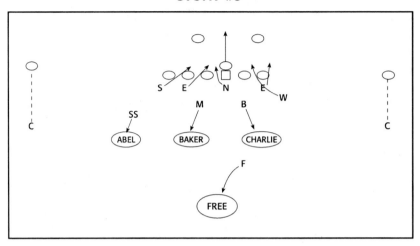

STUNT DESCRIPTION: This **fire zone blitz** has both outside linebackers rushing.

SECONDARY COVERAGE: Cover 1 disguised as cover 3. Mike, Buck, and the strong safety drop off into coverage, and the free safety plays centerfield.

STRONG SAFETY: Lines up as though he's playing cover 3. Keys the tight end. If he blocks, the strong safety quickly supports strongside run. Drops **Abel** versus dropback pass. Checks the tight end for throwback before pursuing weakside run.

STUD: Slants across the tight end's face into the C gap. Secures the C gap and contains the quarterback.

STRONG END: Slants into the B gap.

MIKE: Mike has no strongside gap responsibility. Pursues strongside runs from an inside-out position. Versus weakside runs, checks the weakside A gap as he shuffles down the line. Versus pass, drops **Baker**.

NOSE: Slants through the strongside A gap.

BUCK: Versus weakside run, scrapes outside and contains. Versus strongside run, checks the weakside A gap as he pursues the ball from an inside-out position. Drops **Charlie** versus pass.

WEAK END: Plays 5 technique versus run. Contains the quarterback versus pass.

WHIP: Blitzes through the B gap.

FREE SAFETY: Free. Plays centerfield. Provides alley support versus run.

STRONG CORNER: Plays cover 1. Inside/outside technique is dependent upon field position and the distance of the flanker's split.

WEAK CORNER: Plays cover 1. Inside/outside technique is dependent upon field position and the distance of the split end's split.

STUNT #4

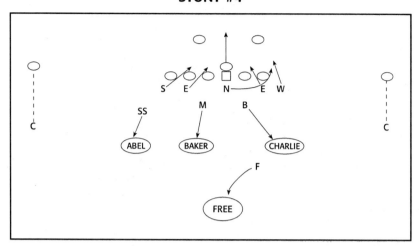

STUNT DESCRIPTION: This **fire zone blitz** has both outside linebackers rushing.

SECONDARY COVERAGE: Cover 1 disguised as cover 3. Mike, Buck, and the strong safety drop off into coverage, and the free safety plays centerfield.

STRONG SAFETY: Lines up as though he's playing cover 3. Keys the tight end. If he blocks, the strong safety quickly supports strongside run. Drops **Abel** versus dropback pass. Checks the tight end for throwback before pursuing weakside run.

STUD: Slants across the tight end's face into the C gap. Secures the C gap and contains the quarterback.

STRONG END: Slants into the B gap.

MIKE: Mike has no strongside gap responsibility. Pursues strongside runs from an inside-out position. Versus weakside runs, checks the weakside A gap as he shuffles down the line. Versus pass, drops **Baker**.

NOSE: Loops across the face of the offensive tackle and secures the weakside C gap.

BUCK: Pursues the ball from an inside-out position versus weakside run. Versus strongside run, checks both A gaps as he shuffles down the line. Drops **Charlie** versus pass.

WEAK END: Slants into the B gap.

WHIP: Rushes from the edge. Contains the quarterback and weakside run. Chases strongside run.

FREE SAFETY: Free. Plays centerfield. Provides alley support versus run.

STRONG CORNER: Plays cover 1. Inside/outside technique is dependent upon field position and the distance of the flanker's split.

WEAK CORNER: Plays cover 1. Inside/outside technique is dependent upon field position and the distance of the split end's split.

STUNT #5

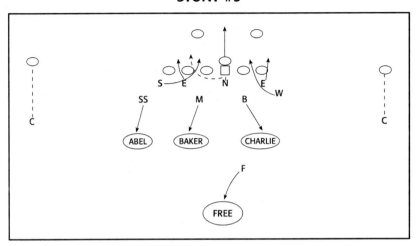

STUNT DESCRIPTION: This **fire zone blitz** has both outside linebackers rushing. This stunt is enhanced by a delayed line twist (twin stunt) by the nose.

SECONDARY COVERAGE: Cover 1 disguised as cover 3. Mike, Buck, and the strong safety drop off into coverage, and the free safety plays centerfield.

STRONG SAFETY: Lines up as though he's playing cover 3. Keys the tight end. If he blocks, the strong safety quickly supports strongside run. Drops **Abel** versus dropback pass. Checks the tight end for throwback before pursuing weakside run.

STUD: Loops through the B gap.

STRONG END: Penetrates through the C gap at the snap. Secures the C gap and contains the quarterback.

MIKE: Has no strongside or wekside gap responsibility. Pursues run from an inside-out position. Versus pass, drops **Baker**.

NOSE: Plays 0 technique versus run. Versus pass, slants across the face of the offensive guard into the strongside B gap (twin stunt).

BUCK: Versus weakside run, scrapes outside and contains. Versus strongside run, pursues the ball from an inside-out position. Drops **Charlie** versus pass.

WEAK END: Plays 5 technique versus run. Contains the quarterback versus pass.

WHIP: Blitzes through the B gap.

FREE SAFETY: Free. Plays centerfield. Provides alley support versus run.

STRONG CORNER: Plays cover 1. Inside/outside technique is dependent upon field position and the distance of the flanker's split.

WEAK CORNER: Plays cover 1. Inside/outside technique is dependent upon field position and the distance of the split end's split.

STUNT #6

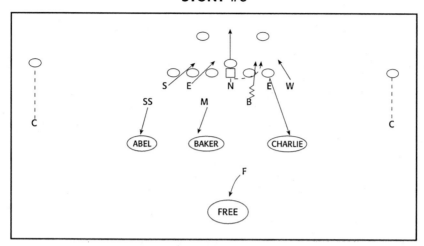

STUNT DESCRIPTION: This **fire zone blitz** has both outside linebackers and Buck rushing and the nose executing a delayed twin rush versus pass.

SECONDARY COVERAGE: Cover 1 disguised as cover 3. Mike, the strong safety, and the weak end drop off into coverage, and the free safety plays centerfield.

STRONG SAFETY: Lines up as though he's playing cover 3. Keys the tight end. If he blocks, the strong safety quickly supports strongside run. Drops **Abel** versus dropback pass. Checks the tight end for throwback before pursuing weakside run.

STUD: Slants across the face of the tight end. Secures the C gap and contains the quarterback.

STRONG END: Slants into the B gap.

MIKE: Has no gap responsibility. Pursues strongside and weakside runs from an inside-out position. Versus pass, drops **Baker**.

NOSE: Plays 0 technique versus run. Slants across the offensive guard's face into the weakside B gap (twin stunt) versus pass.

BUCK: Creeps toward the line during cadence and blitzes through the outside shoulder of the offensive guard at the snap.

WEAK END: Plays 5 technique versus run. Drops **Charlie** versus pass.

WHIP: Rushes from the edge. Contains the quarterback and weakside run. Chases strongside run.

FREE SAFETY: Free. Plays centerfield. Provides alley support versus run.

STRONG CORNER: Plays cover 1. Inside/outside technique is dependent upon field position and the distance of the flanker's split.

WEAK CORNER: Plays cover 1. Inside/outside technique is dependent upon field position and the distance of the split end's split.

STUNT #7

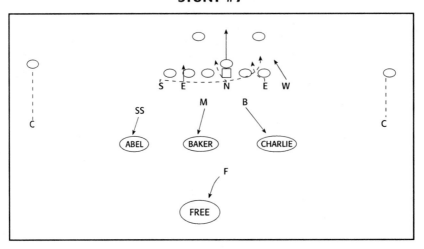

STUNT DESCRIPTION: This **fire zone blitz** sends Whip and features a delayed line twist by Stud versus pass.

SECONDARY COVERAGE: Cover 1 disguised as cover 3. Mike, Buck, and the strong safety drop off into coverage, and the free safety plays centerfield.

STRONG SAFETY: Lines up as though he's playing cover 3. Keys the tight end. If he blocks, the strong safety quickly supports strongside run. Drops **Abel** versus dropback pass. Checks the tight end for throwback before pursuing weakside run.

STUD: Plays 9 technique versus run. Versus pass, loops into the weakside B gap (twin stunt).

STRONG END: Penetrates the C gap at the snap. Secures the C gap and contains the quarterback.

MIKE: Plays base technique versus run. Drops **Baker** versus pass.

NOSE: Plays 0 technique versus run. Versus pass, quickly penetrates the strongside A gap.

BUCK: Plays base technique versus run. Drops **Charlie** versus pass.

WEAK END: Plays 5 technique versus run. Versus pass, slants across the tackle's face and penetrates the B gap.

WHIP: Rushes from the edge. Contains the quarterback and weakside run. Chases strongside run.

FREE SAFETY: Free. Plays centerfield. Provides alley support versus run.

STRONG CORNER: Plays cover 1. Inside/outside technique is dependent upon field position and the distance of the flanker's split.

WEAK CORNER: Plays cover 1. Inside/outside technique is dependent upon field position and the distance of the split end's split.

STUNT #8

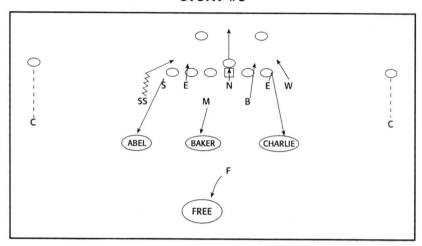

STUNT DESCRIPTION: This **fire zone blitz** has the strong safety rushing from the edge.

SECONDARY COVERAGE: Cover 1 disguised as cover 3. Mike, Stud, and the weak end drop off into coverage versus pass, and the free safety plays centerfield.

STRONG SAFETY: Lines up as though he's playing cover 3 sky. Creeps toward the line during cadence and rushes hard from the edge. Contains the quarterback and strongside runs. Chases weakside runs.

STUD: Plays 9 technique versus run. Drops **Abel** versus pass.

STRONG END: Plays 5 technique.

MIKE: Plays base technique versus run. Versus pass, drops **Baker**.

NOSE: Plays 0 technique.

BUCK: Blitzes through the outside shoulder of the offensive guard and secures the B gap.

WEAK END: Plays 5 technique versus run. Drops **Charlie** versus pass.

WHIP: Rushes from the edge. Contains the quarterback and weakside run. Chases strongside run.

FREE SAFETY: Free. Plays centerfield. Provides alley support versus run.

STRONG CORNER: Plays cover 1. Inside/outside technique is dependent upon field position and the distance of the flanker's split.

WEAK CORNER: Plays cover 1. Inside/outside technique is dependent upon field position and the distance of the split end's split.

STUNT #9

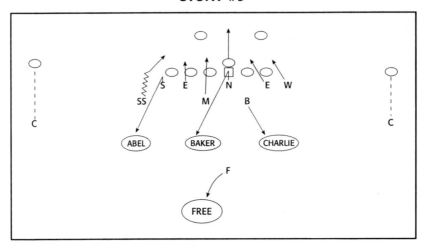

STUNT DESCRIPTION: This **fire zone blitz** has the strong safety rushing from the edge.

SECONDARY COVERAGE: Cover 1 disguised as cover 3. Stud, nose, and Buck drop off into coverage, and the free safety plays centerfield.

STRONG SAFETY: Lines up as though he's playing cover 3 sky. Creeps toward the line during cadence and rushes hard from the edge. Contains the quarterback and strongside runs. Chases weakside runs.

STUD: Plays 9 technique versus run. Drops **Abel** versus pass.

LEFT END: Plays 5 technique.

MIKE: Blitzes through the outside shoulder of the offensive guard and secures the B gap.

NOSE: Plays 0 technique versus run. Drops **Baker** versus pass.

BUCK: Buck has no strongside gap responsibility. Versus weakside runs, scrapes outside and contains. Versus pass, drops **Charlie**.

WEAK END: Slants across the offensive tackle's face into the B gap.

WHIP: Rushes through the outside shoulder of the offensive tackle. Secures the C gap and contains the quarterback.

FREE SAFETY: Free. Plays centerfield. Provides alley support versus run.

STRONG CORNER: Plays cover 1. Inside/outside technique is dependent upon field position and the distance of the flanker's split.

WEAK CORNER: Plays cover 1. Inside/outside technique is dependent upon field position and the distance of the split end's split.

STUNT #10

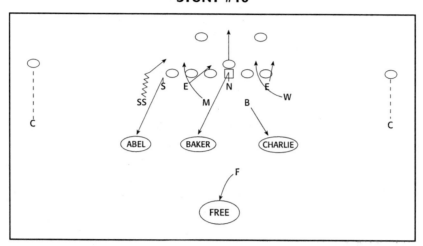

STUNT DESCRIPTION: This **fire zone blitz** has the strong safety rushing from the edge.

SECONDARY COVERAGE: Cover 1 disguised as cover 3. Stud, nose, and Buck drop off into coverage, and the free safety plays centerfield.

STRONG SAFETY: Lines up as though he's playing cover 3 sky. Creeps toward the line during cadence and rushes hard from the edge. Contains the quarterback and strongside runs. Chases weakside runs.

STUD: Plays 9 technique versus run. Drops **Abel** versus pass.

STRONG END: Slants across the offensive tackle's face into the B gap.

MIKE: Blitzes through the outside shoulder of the offensive tackle and secures the C gap.

NOSE: Plays 0 technique versus run. Drops **Baker** versus pass.

BUCK: Versus weakside run, scrapes outside and contains. Pursues strongside run from an inside-out position. Drops **Charlie** versus pass.

WEAK END: Plays 5 technique versus run. Contains the quarterback versus pass.

WHIP: Blitzes through the B gap.

FREE SAFETY: Free. Plays centerfield. Provides alley support versus run.

STRONG CORNER: Plays cover 1. Inside/outside technique is dependent upon field position and the distance of the flanker's split.

WEAK CORNER: Plays cover 1. Inside/outside technique is dependent upon field position and the distance of the split end's split.

STUNT #11

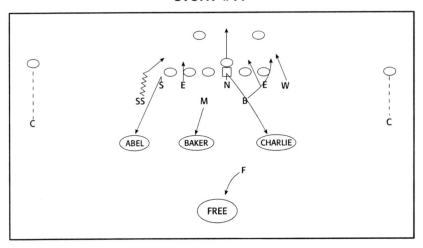

STUNT DESCRIPTION: This **fire zone blitz** has the strong safety rushing from the edge.

SECONDARY COVERAGE: Cover 1 disguised as cover 3. Stud, Mike, and nose drop off into coverage, and the free safety plays centerfield.

STRONG SAFETY: Lines up as though he's playing cover 3 sky. Creeps toward the line during cadence and rushes hard from the edge. Contains the quarterback and strongside runs. Chases weakside runs.

STUD: Plays 9 technique versus run. Drops **Abel** versus pass.

STRONG END: Plays 5 technique.

MIKE: Plays base technique versus run. Drops **Baker** versus pass.

NOSE: Plays 0 technique versus run. Drops **Charlie** versus pass.

BUCK: Blitzes through the outside shoulder of the offensive tackle and secures the C gap.

WEAK END: Slants across the offensive tackle's face into the B gap.

WHIP: Rushes hard from the edge. Contains the quarterback and weakside runs. Chases strongside runs.

FREE SAFETY: Free. Plays centerfield. Provides alley support versus run.

STRONG CORNER: Plays cover 1. Inside/outside technique is dependent upon field position and the distance of the flanker's split.

WEAK CORNER: Plays cover 1. Inside/outside technique is dependent upon field position and the distance of the split end's split.

STUNT #12

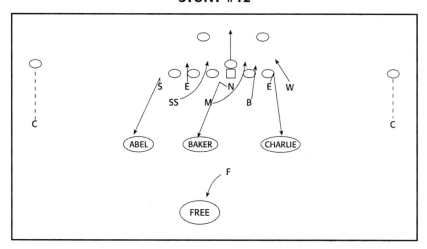

STUNT DESCRIPTION: This **fire zone blitz** puts intense inside pressure on the quarterback.

SECONDARY COVERAGE: Cover 1. Stud, nose and the weak end drop off in coverage, and the free safety plays centerfield.

STRONG SAFETY: Lines up inside shade on the tight end, 4 to 5 yards deep. Blitzes through the B gap at the snap.

STUD: Plays 8 technique versus run. Drops **Abel** versus pass.

STRONG END: Plays 5 technique versus run. Contains the quarterback versus pass.

MIKE: Blitzes through the weakside A gap.

NOSE: Slants to and secures the strongside A gap versus run and drops **Baker** versus pass.

BUCK: Blitzes through the outside shoulder of the offensive guard and secures the B gap.

WEAK END: Plays 5 technique versus run. Drops **Charlie** versus pass.

WHIP: Rushes from the edge. Contains the quarterback and strongside runs. Chases weakside runs.

FREE SAFETY: Free. Plays centerfield. Provides alley support versus run.

STRONG CORNER: Plays cover 1. Inside/outside technique is dependent upon field position and the distance of the flanker's split.

WEAK CORNER: Plays cover 1. Inside/outside technique is dependent upon field position and the distance of the split end's split.

STUNT #13

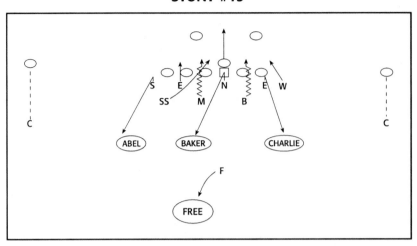

STUNT DESCRIPTION: This **fire zone blitz** features a strong safety blitz and a twin stunt through the strongside B gap.

SECONDAY COVERAGE: Cover 1. Stud, nose, and the weak end drop off into coverage, and the free safety is free.

STRONG SAFETY: Lines up inside shade on the tight end, 4 to 5 yards deep. Blitzes through the B gap at the snap.

STUD: Plays 8 technique versus run. Drops **Abel** versus pass.

STRONG END: Plays 5 technique versus run. Contains the quarterback versus pass.

MIKE: Creeps toward the line during cadence and blitzes through the outside shoulder of the guard at the snap.

NOSE: Plays 0 technique versus run. Drops **Baker** versus pass.

BUCK: Creeps toward the line during cadence and blitzes through the outside shoulder of the offensive guard. Secures the B gap.

WEAK END: Plays 5 technique versus run. Drops **Charlie** versus pass.

WHIP: Rushes from the edge. Contains the quarterback and weakside runs. Chases strongside runs.

FREE SAFETY: Free. Plays centerfield. Provides alley support versus run.

STRONG CORNER: Plays cover 1. Inside/outside technique is dependent upon field position and the distance of the flanker's split.

WEAK CORNER: Plays cover 1. Inside/outside technique is dependent upon field position and the distance of the split end's split.

STUNT #14

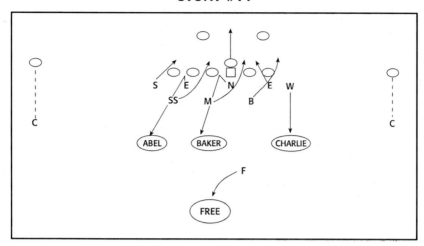

STUNT DESCRIPTION: This **fire zone blitz** gives the initial illusion of an 8-man pass rush.

SECONDARY COVERAGE: Cover 1. The strong end, nose, and Whip drop off into coverage, and the free safety is free.

STRONG SAFETY: Lines up on inside shade of the tight end, 4 to 5 yards deep. Blitzes through the B gap.

STUD: Lines up in an 8 technique. Rushes hard from the outside. Contains the quarterback and strongside runs. Chases weakside runs.

STRONG END: Plays 5 technique versus run. Drops **Abel** versus pass.

MIKE: Blitzes through the weakside A gap.

NOSE: Slants to and secures the strongside A gap versus run. Drops **Baker** versus pass.

BUCK: Blitzes through the outside shoulder of the offensive tackle. Secures the C gap and contains the quarterback.

WEAK END: Slants across the face of the offensive tackle into the B gap.

WHIP: Plays 9 technique versus run. Drops **Charlie** versus pass.

FREE SAFETY: Free. Plays centerfield. Provides alley support versus run.

STRONG CORNER: Plays cover 1. Inside/outside technique is dependent upon field position and the distance of the flanker's split.

WEAK CORNER: Plays cover 1. Inside/outside technique is dependent upon field position and the distance of the split end's split.

STUNT #15

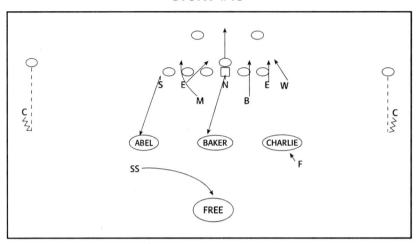

STUNT DESCRIPTION: This **fire zone blitz** gives the initial illusion of a 7-man pass rush.

SECONDARY COVERAGE: Cover 1 disguised as cover 2. Stud, nose and the free safety drop off into coverage, and the strong safety is free.

STRONG SAFETY: Lines up as though he's playing cover 2. Versus pass, drops to centerfield. Versus strongside run, comes up quickly and contains. Versus weakside run, checks throw back first, and then pursues.

STUD: Plays 9 technique versus run. Drops **Abel** versus pass.

STRONG END: Slants into the B gap.

MIKE: Blitzes through the outside shoulder of the offensive tackle. Secures the C gap and contains the quarterback.

NOSE: Plays 0 technique versus run. Drops **Baker** versus pass.

BUCK: Blitzes through the outside shoulder of the offensive guard and secures the B gap.

WEAK END: Plays 5 technique.

WHIP: Rushes from the edge. Contains the quarterback and weakside runs. Chases strongside runs.

FREE SAFETY: Lines up as though he's playing cover 2. Versus pass, drops **Charlie**. Versus weakside run, comes up quickly and helps contain. Versus strongside run, checks throwback first and then pursues.

STRONG CORNER: Plays cover 1. Gives the quarterback a cover 2 pre-snap read. Inside/outside technique is dependent upon field position and the distance of the flanker's split.

WEAK CORNER: Plays cover 1. Gives the quarterback a cover 2 pre-snap read. Inside/outside technique is dependent upon field position and the distance of the split end's split.

STUNT #16

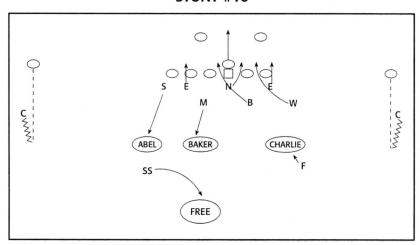

STUNT DESCRIPTION: This **fire zone blitz** sends Buck and Whip.

SECONDARY COVERAGE: Cover 1 disguised as cover 2. Stud, Mike, and the free safety drop off into coverage, and the strong safety is free.

STRONG SAFETY: Lines up as though he's playing cover 2. Versus pass, drops to centerfield. Versus strongside run, comes up quickly and contains. Versus weakside run, checks throwback first and then pursues.

STUD: Plays 9 technique versus run. Drops **Abel** versus pass.

STRONG END: Plays 5 technique versus run. Contains the quarterback versus pass.

MIKE: Plays base technique versus run. Drops **Baker** versus pass.

NOSE: Slants into the weakside A gap.

BUCK: Blitzes through the strongside A gap.

WEAK END: Slants to and secures the C gap versus run. Contains the quarterback versus pass.

WHIP: Blitzes through the B gap.

FREE SAFETY: Lines up as though he's playing cover 2. Versus pass, drops **Charlie**. Versus weakside run, comes up quickly and helps contain. Versus strongside run, checks throwback first, and then pursues.

STRONG CORNER: Plays cover 1. Gives the quarterback a cover 2 pre-snap read. Inside/outside technique is dependent upon field position and the distance of the flanker's split.

WEAK CORNER: Plays cover 1. Gives the quarterback a cover 2 pre-snap read. Inside/outside technique is dependent upon field position and the distance of the split end's split.

STUNT #17

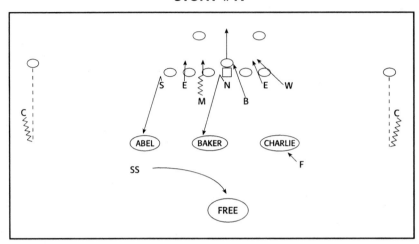

STUNT DESCRIPTION: This **fire zone blitz** gives the initial illusion of a 7-man pass rush.

SECONDARY COVERAGE: Cover 1 disguised as cover 2. Stud, nose, and the free safety drop off into coverage, and the strong safety is free.

STRONG SAFETY: Lines up as though he's playing cover 2. Versus pass, drops to centerfield. Versus strongside run, comes up quickly and contains. Versus weakside run, checks throwback first and then pursues.

STUD: Plays 9 technique versus run. Drops **Abel** versus pass.

STRONG END: Plays 5 technique versus run. Contains the quarterback versus pass.

MIKE: Creeps toward the line during cadence. Blitzes through the outside shoulder of the offensive guard and secures the B gap.

NOSE: Slants to and secures the strongside A gap versus run and drops **Baker** versus pass.

BUCK: Blitzes through the weakside A gap.

WEAK END: Slants across the face of the offensive tackle into the B gap.

WHIP: Blitzes through the outside shoulder of the offensive tackle. Secures the C gap and contains the quarterback.

FREE SAFETY: Lines up as though he's playing cover 2. Versus pass, drops **Charlie**. Versus weakside run, comes up quickly and contains. Versus strongside run, checks throwback first, and then pursues.

STRONG CORNER: Plays cover 1. Gives the quarterback a cover 2 pre-snap read. Inside/outside technique is dependent upon field position and the distance of the flanker's split.

WEAK CORNER: Plays cover 1. Gives the quarterback a cover 2 pre-snap read. Inside/outside technique is dependent upon field position and the distance of the split end's split.

STUNT #18

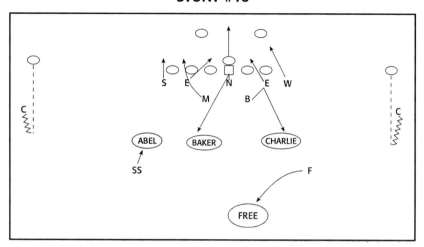

STUNT DESCRIPTION: This **fire zone blitz** gives the initial illusion of a 7-man pass rush.

SECONDARY COVERAGE: Cover 1 disguised as cover 2. The strong safety, nose, and Buck drop off into coverage, and the free safety is free.

STRONG SAFETY: Lines up as though he's playing cover 2. Versus pass, drops **Abel**. Versus strongside run, comes up quickly and contains. Versus weakside run, checks throwback first, and then pursues.

STUD: Plays 9 technique versus run. Contains the quarterback versus pass.

STRONG END: Slants across the offensive tackle's face into the B gap.

MIKE: Blitzes through the outside shoulder of the offensive tackle and secures the C gap.

NOSE: Plays 0 technique versus run. Drops **Baker** versus pass.

BUCK: Fakes a blitz toward the C gap. Secures C gap versus run and drops **Charlie** versus pass.

WEAK END: Slants across the face of the offensive tackle into the B gap.

WHIP: Rushes from the edge. Contains the quarterback and strongside runs. Chases weakside runs.

FREE SAFETY: Lines up as though he's playing cover 2. Versus pass, drops to centerfield. Versus weakside run, comes up quickly and contains. Versus strongside run, checks throwback first, and then pursues.

STRONG CORNER: Plays cover 1. Gives the quarterback a cover 2 pre-snap read. Inside/ outside technique is dependent upon field position and the distance of the flanker's split.

WEAK CORNER: Plays cover 1. Gives the quarterback a cover 2 pre-snap read. Inside/ outside technique is dependent upon field position and the distance of the split end's split.

STUNT #19

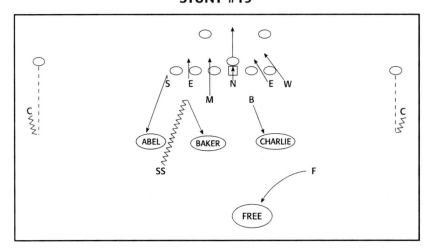

STUNT DESCRIPTION: This **fire zone blitz** features a fake strong safety blitz.

SECONDARY COVERAGE: Cover 1 disguised as cover 2. The strong safety, Stud, and Buck drop off into coverage, and the free safety is free.

STRONG SAFETY: Lines up as though he's playing cover 2. Creeps toward the line during cadence and convinces the quarterback that he intends to blitz inside. Versus pass, drops **Baker**. Contains strongside runs and checks the tight end before pursuing weakside runs.

STUD: Plays 9 technique versus run. Drops **Abel** versus pass.

STRONG END: Plays 5 technique versus run. Contains the quarterback versus pass.

MIKE: Blitzes through the outside shoulder of the offensive guard and secures the B gap.

NOSE: Plays 0 technique.

BUCK: Versus weakside run, scrapes outside and contains. Pursues strongside runs from an inside-out position. Drops **Charlie** versus pass.

WEAK END: Slants across the face of the offensive tackle into the B gap.

WHIP: Rushes through the outside shoulder of the offensive tackle. Secures the C gap and contains the quarterback.

FREE SAFETY: Lines up as though he's playing cover 2. Versus pass, drops to centerfield. Versus weakside run, comes up quickly and contains. Versus strongside run, checks throwback first, and then pursues.

STRONG CORNER: Plays cover 1. Gives the quarterback a cover 2 pre-snap read. Inside/outside technique is dependent upon field position and the distance of the flanker's split.

WEAK CORNER: Plays cover 1. Gives the quarterback a cover 2 pre-snap read. Inside/outside technique is dependent upon field position and the distance of the split end's split.

STUNT #20

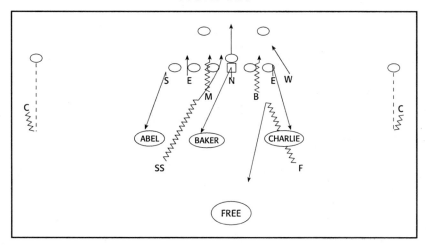

STUNT DESCRIPTION: This **fire zone blitz** features a strong safety blitz. It also gives the offense the pre-snap read that the defense is "sending the house."

SECONDARY COVERAGE: Cover 1 disguised as cover 2. Stud and nose drop off into coverage, and the weak end spies the near back. The free safety is free.

STRONG SAFETY: Lines up as though he's playing cover 2. Quickly moves toward the line during cadence and blitzes through the strongside A gap.

STUD: Plays 9 technique versus run. Drops **Abel** versus pass.

STRONG END: Penetrates the C gap at the snap. Secures the C gap and contains the quarterback.

MIKE: Creeps toward the line during cadence and blitzes through the outside shoulder of the offensive guard at the snap. Secures the B gap.

NOSE: Plays 0 technique versus run. Drops **Baker** versus pass.

BUCK: Creeps toward the line during cadence and blitzes through the outside shoulder of the offensive guard at the snap. Secures the B gap.

WEAK END: Plays 5 technique versus run. Drops **Charlie** versus pass.

WHIP: Rushes from the edge. Contains the quarterback and strongside runs. Chases weakside runs.

FREE SAFETY: Lines up as though he's playing cover 2. Creeps toward the line during cadence and convinces the quarterback that a double safety blitz is in progress. Versus pass, drops to centerfield. Versus weakside run, comes up quickly and contains. Versus strongside run, checks throwback first, and then pursues.

STRONG CORNER: Plays cover 1. Gives the quarterback a cover 2 pre-snap read. Inside/outside technique is dependent upon field position and the distance of the flanker's split.

WEAK CORNER: Plays cover 1. Gives the quarterback a cover 2 pre-snap read. Inside/outside technique is dependent upon field position and the distance of the split end's split.

STUNT #21

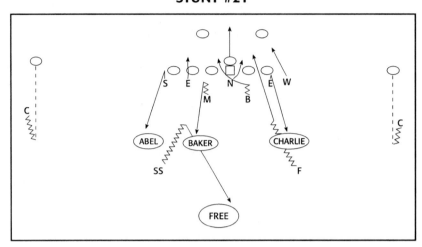

STUNT DESCRIPTION: This **fire zone blitz** features a weak safety blitz and gives the quarterback the illusion that the defense is "sending the house."

SECONDARY COVERAGE: Cover 1 disguised as cover 2. Stud, nose, and the weak end drop off into coverage, and the strong safety is free.

STRONG SAFETY: Lines up as though he's playing cover 2. Creeps toward the line during cadence and convinces the quarterback that a double safety blitz is in progress. Versus pass, drops to centerfield. Versus strongside run, comes up quickly and contains. Checks the tight end before pursuing weakside run.

STUD: Plays 9 technique versus run. Drops **Abel** versus pass.

STRONG END: Plays 5 technique versus run. Contains the quarterback versus pass.

MIKE: Creeps toward the line during cadence and "shows blitz." Secures the B gap versus run and drops **Baker** versus pass.

NOSE: Slants into the weakside A gap.

BUCK: Creeps toward the line as though he's going to blitz through the outside shoulder of the guard. Blitzes through the strongside A gap as the ball is being snapped.

WEAK END: Plays 5 technique versus run. Drops **Charlie** versus pass.

WHIP: Rushes from the edge. Contains the quarterback and strongside runs. Chases weakside runs.

FREE SAFETY: Lines up as though he's playing cover 2. Quickly moves toward the line during cadence and blitzes through the weakside B gap.

STRONG CORNER: Plays cover 1. Gives the quarterback a cover 2 pre-snap read. Inside/outside technique is dependent upon field position and the distance of the flanker's split.

WEAK CORNER: Plays cover 1. Gives the quarterback a cover 2 pre-snap read. Inside/outside technique is dependent upon field position and the distance of the split end's split.

STUNT #22

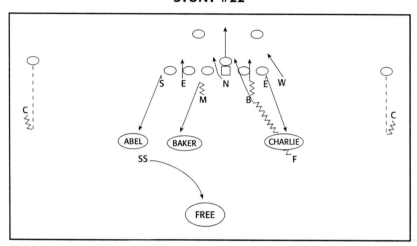

STUNT DESCRIPTION: This **fire zone blitz** features a free safety blitz.

SECONDARY COVERAGE: Cover 1 disguised as cover 2. Stud, Mike, and the weak end drop off into coverage, and the strong safety is free.

STRONG SAFETY: Lines up as though he's playing cover 2. Versus pass, drops to centerfield. Versus strongside run, comes up quickly and contains. Checks the tight end before pursuing weakside run.

STUD: Plays 9 technique versus run. Drops **Abel** versus pass.

STRONG END: Plays 5 technique versus run. Contains the quarterback versus pass.

MIKE: Creeps toward the line during cadence and "shows blitz." Secures the B gap versus run and drops **Baker** versus pass.

NOSE: Slants into the strongside A gap.

BUCK: Creeps toward the line and blitzes through the outside shoulder of the guard. Secures the B gap.

WEAK END: Plays 5 technique versus run. Drops **Charlie** versus pass.

WHIP: Rushes from the edge. Contains the quarterback and strongside runs. Chases weakside runs.

FREE SAFETY: Lines up as though he's playing cover 2. Quickly moves toward the line during cadence and blitzes through the weakside A gap.

STRONG CORNER: Plays cover 1. Gives the quarterback a cover 2 pre-snap read. Inside/ outside technique is dependent upon field position and the distance of the flanker's split.

WEAK CORNER: Plays cover 1. Gives the quarterback a cover 2 pre-snap read. Inside/ outside technique is dependent upon field position and the distance of the split end's split.

STUNT #23

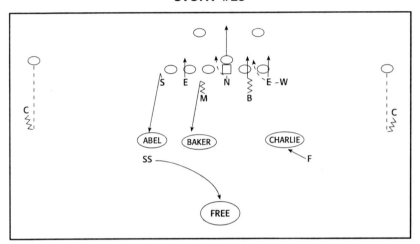

STUNT DESCRIPTION: This **fire zone blitz** features a delayed twin stunt through the weakside B gap.

SECONDARY COVERAGE: Cover 1 disguised as cover 2. Stud, Mike, and the free safety drop off into coverage, and the strong safety is free.

STRONG SAFETY: Lines up as though he's playing cover 2. Versus pass, drops to centerfield. Versus strongside run, comes up quickly and contains. Checks the tight end before pursuing weakside run.

STUD: Plays 9 technique versus run. Drops **Abel** versus pass.

STRONG END: Plays 5 technique versus run. Contains the quarterback versus pass.

MIKE: Creeps toward the line during cadence and "shows blitz." Secures the B gap versus run and drops **Baker** versus pass.

NOSE: Plays 0 technique versus run. Delay rushes through the strongside A gap (after engaging the center's block) versus pass.

BUCK: Creeps toward the line and blitzes through the outside shoulder of the guard. Secures the B gap.

WEAK END: Plays 5 technique versus run. Contains the quarterback versus pass.

WHIP: Cheats back slightly. Plays 9 technique versus run. Versus pass, delay blitzes (twin stunt) through the weakside B gap.

FREE SAFETY: Lines up as though he's playing cover 2. Versus dropback pass, drops **Charlie**. Versus weakside run, comes up quickly and contains. Versus strongside run, checks throwback before pursuing.

STRONG CORNER: Plays cover 1. Gives the quarterback a cover 2 pre-snap read. Inside/outside technique is dependent upon field position and the distance of the flanker's split.

WEAK CORNER: Plays cover 1. Gives the quarterback a cover 2 pre-snap read. Inside/outside technique is dependent upon field position and the distance of the split end's split.

STUNT #24

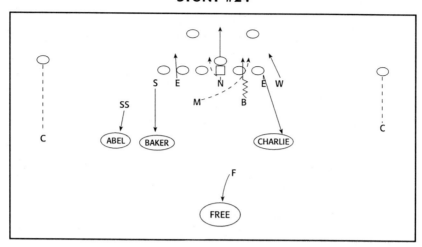

STUNT DESCRIPTION: This **fire zone blitz** features a delayed twin stunt through the weakside B gap.

SECONDARY COVERAGE: Cover 1 disguised as cover 3. The strong safety, Stud, and the weak end drop off into coverage, and the free safety is free.

STRONG SAFETY: Lines up as though he's playing cover 3. Keys the tight end. If he blocks, the strong safety comes up quickly and contains. If he releases, the strong safety drops **Abel**. Checks the tight end before pursuing weakside run.

STUD: Plays 9 technique versus run. Drops **Baker** versus pass.

STRONG END: Plays 5 technique versus run. Contains the quarterback versus pass.

MIKE: Plays base technique versus run. Delay blitzes through the weakside A gap (twin stunt) versus pass.

NOSE: Plays 0 technique versus run. Delay rushes through the strongside A gap (after engaging the center's block) versus pass.

BUCK: Creeps toward the line and blitzes through the outside shoulder of the guard. Secures the B gap.

WEAK END: Plays 5 technique versus run. Drops **Charlie** versus pass.

WHIP: Rushes from the edge. Contains the quarterback and strongside runs. Chases weakside runs.

FREE SAFETY: Free versus pass. Provides alley support versus run.

STRONG CORNER: Plays cover 1. Inside/outside technique is dependent upon field position and the distance of the flanker's split.

WEAK CORNER: Plays cover 1. Inside/outside technique is dependent upon field position and the distance of the split end's split.

STUNT #25

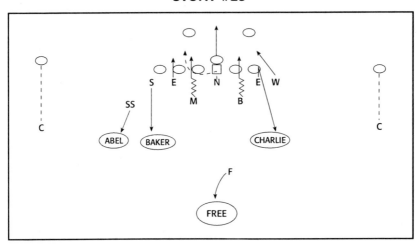

STUNT DESCRIPTION: This **fire zone blitz** gives the offense the initial illusion of a 7-man pass rush and features a delayed twin stunt by the nose.

SECONDARY COVERAGE: Cover 1 disguised as cover 3. The strong safety, Stud, and the weak end drop into coverage and the free safety is free.

STRONG SAFETY: Lines up as though he's playing cover 3. Keys the tight end. If he blocks, the strong safety comes up quickly and contains. If he releases, the strong safety drops **Abel**.

STUD: Plays 9 technique versus run. Drops **Baker** versus pass.

STRONG END: Plays 5 technique versus run. Contains the quarterback versus pass.

MIKE: Creeps toward the line during cadence and blitzes through the outside shoulder of the offensive guard.

NOSE: Plays 0 technique versus run. Delay rushes through the strongside B gap (twin stunt) versus pass.

BUCK: Creeps toward the line and blitzes through the outside shoulder of the guard. Secures the B gap.

WEAK END: Plays 5 technique versus run. Drops **Charlie** versus pass.

WHIP: Rushes from the edge. Contains the quarterback and strongside runs. Chases weakside runs.

FREE SAFETY: Free versus pass. Provides alley support versus pass.

STRONG CORNER: Plays cover 1. Inside/outside technique is dependent upon field position and the distance of the flanker's split.

WEAK CORNER: Plays cover 1. Inside/outside technique is dependent upon field position and the distance of the split end's split.

STUNT #26

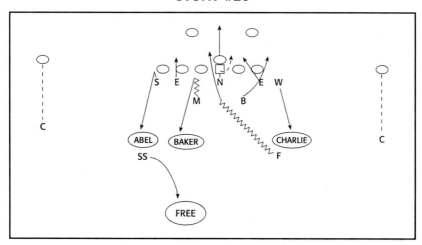

STUNT DESCRIPTION: This **fire zone blitz** features a free safety blitz.

SECONDARY COVERAGE: Cover 1 disguised as cover 2. Stud, Mike, and Whip drop off into coverage, and the strong safety is free.

STRONG SAFETY: Lines up as though he's playing cover 2. Versus pass, drops to centerfield. Versus strongside run, comes up quickly and contains. Checks the tight end before pursuing weakside run.

STUD: Plays 9 technique versus run. Drops **Abel** versus pass.

STRONG END: Plays 5 technique versus run. Contains the quarterback versus pass.

MIKE: Creeps toward the line during cadence and "shows blitz." Secures the B gap versus run and drops **Baker** versus pass.

NOSE: Slants into the weakside A gap.

BUCK: Blitzes through the outside shoulder of the offensive tackle and secures the C gap. Contains the quarterback versus pass.

WEAK END: Slants across the offensive tackle's face into the B gap.

WHIP: Plays 9 technique versus run. Drops **Charlie** versus pass.

FREE SAFETY: Lines up as though he's playing cover 2. Quickly moves toward the line during cadence and blitzes through the strongside A gap.

STRONG CORNER: Plays cover 1. Gives the quarterback a cover 2, pre-snap read. Inside/outside technique is dependent upon field position and the distance of the flanker's split.

WEAK CORNER: Plays cover 1. Gives the quarterback a cover 2, pre-snap read. Inside/outside technique is dependent upon field position and the distance of the split end's split.

STUNT #27

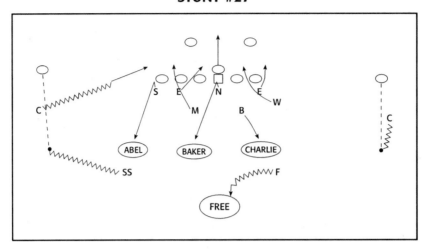

STUNT DESCRIPTION: This **fire zone blitz** features a strong cornerback blitz.

SECONDARY COVERAGE: Cover 1 disguised as cover 2. Stud, nose, and Buck drop off into coverage, and the free safety is free.

STRONG SAFETY: Lines up as though he's playing cover 2. During cadence, moves to a position that enables him to cover the flanker.

STUD: Plays 9 technique versus run. Drops **Abel** versus pass.

STRONG END: Slants across the offensive tackle's face into the B gap.

MIKE: Blitzes through the outside shoulder of the offensive tackle, secures the C gap, and contains the quarterback.

NOSE: Plays 0 technique versus run. Drops **Baker** versus pass.

BUCK: Versus weakside run, scrapes outside and contains. Pursues strongside run from an inside-out position. Drops **Charlie** versus pass.

WEAK END: Slants into the C gap. Secures C gap and contains the quarterback.

WHIP: Cheats back slightly and blitzes through the B gap.

FREE SAFETY: Gives the quarterback a cover 2, pre-snap read. Plays centerfield versus pass, and provides alley support versus run.

STRONG CORNER: Gives the quarterback a cover 2, pre-snap read. Creeps inside during cadence and rushes from the edge. Contains the quarterback and strongside runs. Chases weakside runs.

WEAK CORNER: Plays cover 1. Gives the quarterback a cover 2, pre-snap read. Inside/ outside technique is dependent upon field position and the distance of the split end's split.

STUNT #28

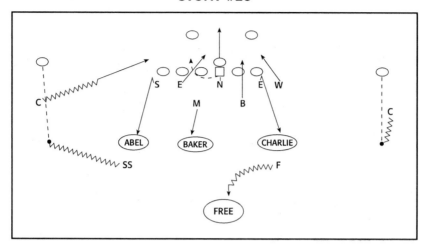

STUNT DESCRIPTION: This **fire zone blitz** features a strong cornerback blitz and a twin stunt through the strongside B gap.

SECONDARY COVERAGE: Cover 1 disguised as cover 2. Stud, Mike, and the weak end drop off into coverage, and the free safety is free.

STRONG SAFETY: Lines up as though he's playing cover 2. During cadence, moves to a position that enables him to cover the flanker.

STUD: Plays 9 technique versus run. Drops **Abel** versus pass.

STRONG END: Slants across the offensive tackle's face into the B gap.

MIKE: Versus strongside runs, scrapes into the C gap. Pursues weakside runs from an inside-out position. Drops **Baker** versus pass.

NOSE: Plays 0 technique versus run. Versus pass, delay rushes (twin stunt) through the strongside B gap.

BUCK: Blitzes through the outside shoulder of the offensive guard and secures the B gap.

WEAK END: Plays 5 technique versus run. Drops **Charlie** versus pass.

WHIP: Rushes from the edge. Contains the quarterback and weakside runs. Chases strongside runs.

FREE SAFETY: Gives the quarterback a cover 2, pre-snap read. Plays centerfield versus pass, and provides alley support versus run.

STRONG CORNER: Gives the quarterback a cover 2, pre-snap read. Creeps inside during cadence and rushes from the edge. Contains the quarterback and strongside runs. Chases weakside runs.

WEAK CORNER: Plays cover 1. Gives the quarterback a cover 2, pre-snap read. Inside/outside technique is dependent upon field position and the distance of the split end's split.

STUNT #29

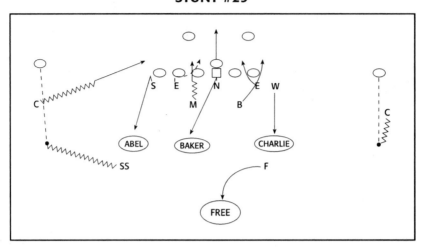

STUNT DESCRIPTION: This **fire zone blitz** features a strong cornerback blitz and a twin stunt through the strongside B gap.

SECONDARY COVERAGE: Cover 1 disguised as cover 2. Stud, nose, and Whip drop off into coverage, and the free safety is free.

STRONG SAFETY: Lines up as though he's playing cover 2. During cadence, moves to a position that enables him to cover the flanker.

STUD: Plays 9 technique versus run. Drops **Abel** versus pass.

STRONG END: Plays 5 technique versus run. Slants behind Mike through the B gap versus pass.

MIKE: Creeps toward the line during cadence and blitzes through the outside shoulder of the offensive guard.

NOSE: Plays 0 technique versus run. Drops **Baker** versus pass.

BUCK: Blitzes through the outside shoulder of the offensive tackle, secures the C gap, and contains the quarterback.

WEAK END: Slants through the outside shoulder of the offensive guard and secures the B gap.

WHIP: Plays 9 technique versus run. Drops **Charlie** versus pass.

FREE SAFETY: Gives the quarterback a cover 2, pre-snap read. Plays centerfield versus pass, and provides alley support versus run.

STRONG CORNER: Gives the quarterback a cover 2, pre-snap read. Creeps inside during cadence and rushes from the edge. Contains the quarterback and strongside runs. Chases weakside runs.

WEAK CORNER: Plays cover 1. Gives the quarterback a cover 2, pre-snap read. Inside/outside technique is dependent upon field position and the distance of the split end's split.

STUNT #30

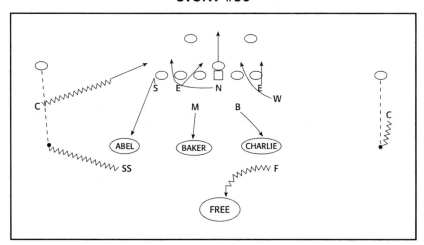

STUNT DESCRIPTION: This **fire zone blitz** features a strong cornerback blitz.

SECONDARY COVERAGE: Cover 1 disguised as cover 2. Stud, Mike and Buck drop off into coverage, and the free safety is free.

STRONG SAFETY: Lines up as though he's playing cover 2. During cadence, moves to a position that enables him to cover the flanker.

STUD: Plays 9 technique versus run. Drops **Abel** versus pass.

STRONG END: Slants across the offensive tackle's face into the B gap.

MIKE: Pursues strongside runs from an inside-out position. Secures the strongside A gap before pursuing weakside runs. Drops **Baker** versus pass.

NOSE: Loops across the offensive tackle's face into the strongside C gap.

BUCK: Versus weakside run, scrapes outside and contains. Checks the strongside A gap as he pursues strongside runs. Drops **Charlie** versus pass.

WEAK END: Plays 5 technique versus run. Contains the quarterback versus pass.

WHIP: Cheats back slightly and blitzes through the B gap.

FREE SAFETY: Gives the quarterback a cover 2, pre-snap read. Plays centerfield versus pass, and provides alley support versus run.

STRONG CORNER: Gives the quarterback a cover 2, pre-snap read. Creeps inside during cadence and rushes from the edge. Contains the quarterback and strongside runs. Chases weakside runs.

WEAK CORNER: Plays cover 1. Gives the quarterback a cover 2, pre-snap read. Inside/outside technique is dependent upon field position and the distance of the split end's split.

STUNT #31

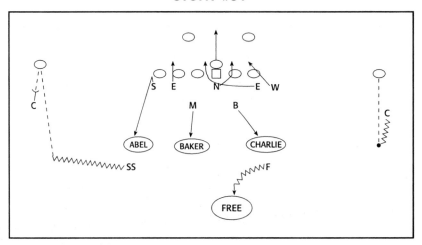

STUNT DESCRIPTION: This **fire zone blitz** features double coverage on the flanker but limits the defense to a 4-man pass rush.

SECONDARY COVERAGE: Cover 1 disguised as cover 2. Stud, Mike and Buck drop off into Banjo coverage, and the free safety is free. The cornerback and the strong safety double cover the flanker.

STRONG SAFETY: Lines up in a cover 2 technique. At the snap, moves to a position that enables him to cover the flanker's deep routes.

STUD: Plays 9 technique versus run. Drops **Abel** versus pass.

STRONG END: Plays 5 technique versus run. Contains the quarterback versus pass.

MIKE: Plays base technique versus run. Drops **Baker** versus pass.

NOSE: Rips through the inside shoulder of the guard and controls the weakside A gap.

BUCK: Versus weakside run, scrapes outside and contains. Pursues strongside runs from an inside-out position. Drops **Charlie** versus pass.

WEAK END: Loops across the face of the center into the strongside A gap.

WHIP: Rushes through the outside shoulder of the offensive tackle. Secures the C gap and contains the quarterback.

FREE SAFETY: Gives the quarterback a cover 2, pre-snap read. Plays centerfield versus pass, and provides alley support versus run.

STRONG CORNER: Gives the quarterback a cover 2, pre-snap read. Jams the flanker and tries to funnel him inside, while covering him man-to-man.

WEAK CORNER: Plays cover 1. Gives the quarterback a cover 2, pre-snap read. Inside/outside technique is dependent upon field position and the distance of the split end's split.

STUNT #32

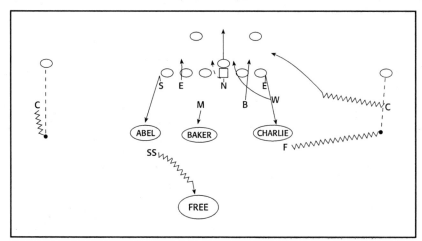

STUNT DESCRIPTION: This **fire zone blitz** features a weak cornerback blitz.

SECONDARY COVERAGE: Cover 1 disguised as cover 2. Stud, Mike, and the weak end drop off into coverage. The strong safety is free.

STRONG SAFETY: Gives the quarterback a cover 2, pre-snap read. During cadence, moves to a position that enables him to play centerfield versus pass and provide alley support versus run.

STUD: Plays 9 technique versus run. Drops **Abel** versus pass.

STRONG END: Plays 5 technique versus run. Contains the quarterback versus pass.

MIKE: Plays base technique versus run. Drops **Baker** versus pass.

NOSE: Plays 0 technique versus run. Rushes through the strongside A gap after engaging the center's block.

BUCK: Blitzes through the outside shoulder of the offensive guard and controls the B gap.

WEAK END: Plays 5 technique versus run. Drops **Charlie** versus pass.

WHIP: Cheats back slightly and blitzes through the weakside A gap.

FREE SAFETY: Gives the quarterback a cover 2, pre-snap read. Moves to a position that enables him to cover the split end as the ball is snapped.

STRONG CORNER: Plays cover 1. Gives the quarterback a cover 2, pre-snap read. Inside/outside technique is dependent upon field position and the distance of the flanker's split.

WEAK CORNER: Gives the quarterback a cover 2, pre-snap read. Creeps inside during cadence and blitzes hard from the edge. Contains the quarterback and weakside runs. Chases strongside runs.

STUNT #33

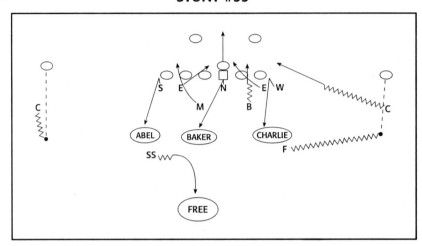

STUNT DESCRIPTION: This **fire zone blitz** features a weak cornerback blitz and a twin stunt through the weakside B gap.

SECONDARY COVERAGE: Cover 1 disguised as cover 2. Stud, Nose, and Whip drop off into coverage, and the strong safety is free.

STRONG SAFETY: Gives the quarterback a cover 2, pre-snap read. During cadence, moves to a position that enables him to play centerfield versus pass and provide alley support versus run.

STUD: Plays 9 technique versus run. Drops **Abel** versus pass.

STRONG END: Slants across the offensive tackle's face into the B gap.

MIKE: Blitzes through the outside shoulder of the offensive tackle. Secures the C gap and contains the quarterback.

NOSE: Plays 0 technique versus run. Drops **Baker** versus pass.

BUCK: Creeps toward the line during cadence and blitzes through the outside shoulder of the offensive guard.

WEAK END: Slants behind Buck through the B gap (twin stunt).

WHIP: Slants to the outside shoulder of the offensive tackle. Secures the C gap versus run and drops **Charlie** versus pass.

FREE SAFETY: Gives the quarterback a cover 2, pre-snap read. Moves to a position that enables him to cover the split end as the ball is snapped.

STRONG CORNER: Plays cover 1. Gives the quarterback a cover 2, pre-snap read. Inside/outside technique is dependent upon field position and the distance of the flanker's split.

WEAK CORNER: Gives the quarterback a cover 2, pre-snap read. Creeps inside during cadence and blitzes hard from the edge. Contains the quarterback and weakside runs. Chases strongside runs.

STUNT #34

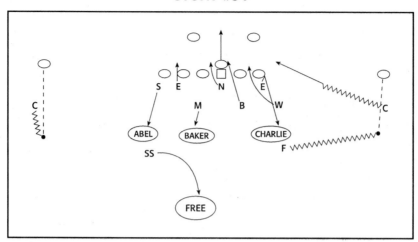

STUNT DESCRIPTION: This **fire zone blitz** features a weak cornerback blitz.

SECONDARY COVERAGE: Cover 1 disguised as cover 2. Stud, Mike, and the weak end drop off into coverage. The strong safety is free.

STRONG SAFETY: Gives the quarterback a cover 2, pre-snap read. During cadence, moves to a position that enables him to play centerfield versus pass and provide alley support versus run.

STUD: Plays 9 technique versus run. Drops **Abel** versus pass.

STRONG END: Plays 5 technique versus run. Contains the quarterback versus pass.

MIKE: Plays base technique versus run. Drops **Baker** versus pass.

NOSE: Slants into the strongside A gap.

BUCK: Blitzes through the weakside A gap.

WEAK END: Plays 5 technique versus run. Drops **Charlie** versus pass.

WHIP: Cheats back slightly and blitzes through the B gap.

FREE SAFETY: Gives the quarterback a cover 2, pre-snap read but moves to a position that enables him to cover the split end as the ball is snapped.

STRONG CORNER: Plays cover 1. Gives the quarterback a cover 2, pre-snap read. Inside/ outside technique is dependent upon field position and the distance of the flanker's split.

WEAK CORNER: Gives the quarterback a cover 2, pre-snap read. Creeps inside during cadence and blitzes hard from the edge. Contains the quarterback and weakside runs. Chases strongside runs.

STUNT #35

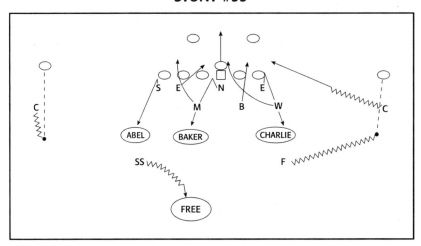

STUNT DESCRIPTION: This **fire zone blitz** gives the initial illusion of an 8-man pass rush.

SECONDARY COVERAGE: Cover 1 disguised as cover 2. Stud, Nose, and the weak end drop off into coverage and the strong safety is free.

STRONG SAFETY: Gives the quarterback a cover 2, pre-snap read. During cadence, moves to a position that enables him to play centerfield versus pass and provide alley support versus.

STUD: Plays 9 technique versus run. Drops **Abel** versus pass.

STRONG END: Plays 5 technique versus run. Contains the quarterback versus pass.

MIKE: Blitzes through the outside shoulder of the offensive tackle, secures the C gap, and contains the quarterback.

NOSE: Slants to and secures the strongside A gap versus run and drops **Baker** versus pass.

BUCK: Blitzes through the B gap.

WEAK END: Plays 5 technique versus run. Drops **Charlie** versus pass.

WHIP: Cheats back slightly and blitzes through the weakside A gap.

FREE SAFETY: Gives the quarterback a cover 2, pre-snap read. During cadence, moves to a position that enables him to cover the split end as the ball is snapped.

STRONG CORNER: Plays cover 1. Gives the quarterback a cover 2, pre-snap read. Inside/outside technique is dependent upon field position and the distance of the flanker's split.

WEAK CORNER: Gives the quarterback a cover 2, pre-snap read. Creeps inside during cadence and blitzes hard from the edge. Contains the quarterback and weakside runs. Chases strongside runs.

STUNT #36

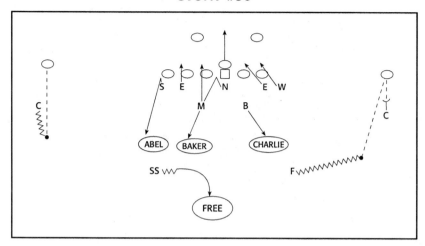

STUNT DESCRIPTION: This **fire zone blitz** provides the defense with double coverage on the split end but reduces the pass rush to four.

SECONDARY COVERAGE: Cover 1 disguised as cover 2 with double coverage on the split end. Stud, Mike, and Buck drop off into coverage, and the strong safety is free.

STRONG SAFETY: Gives the quarterback a cover 2, pre-snap read. During cadence, moves to a position that enables him to play centerfield versus pass, and provide alley support versus run.

STUD: Plays 9 technique versus run. Drops **Abel** versus pass.

STRONG END: Plays 5 technique versus run. Contains the quarterback versus pass.

MIKE: Blitzes through the outside shoulder of the offensive guard and secures the B gap.

NOSE: Slants to and secures the strongside A gap versus run and drops **Baker** versus pass.

BUCK: Versus weakside run, scrapes outside and contains. Checks the weakside A gap as he pursues strongside runs from an inside-out position. Drops **Charlie** versus pass.

WEAK END: Slants across the face of the offensive tackle into the B gap.

WHIP: Rushes through the outside shoulder of the offensive tackle and secures the C gap.

FREE SAFETY: Gives the quarterback a cover 2, pre-snap read. Moves to a position that enables him to cover the split end's deep patterns as the ball is snapped.

STRONG CORNER: Plays cover 1. Gives the quarterback a cover 2, pre-snap read. Inside/outside technique is dependent upon field position and the distance of the flanker's split.

WEAK CORNER: Gives the quarterback a cover 2, pre-snap read. Jams the split end and funnels him inside. Covers him man-to-man.

CHAPTER 6

SPLIT-4
FIRE ZONE BLITZES

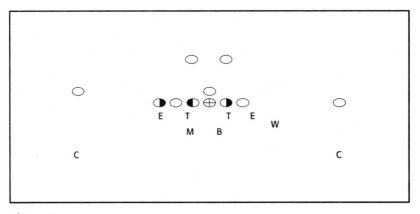

Figure 6-1

Strong cornerback—the cornerback who lines up opposite the flanker.

Assassin—the free safety.

Stud—the outside linebacker who lines up toward the strongside (8 technique).

Strong end—the defensive end who lines up on the strongside (7 technique).

Strong tackle—the defensive tackle who lines up on the strongside (3 technique).

Mike—the inside linebacker aligned on the strongside.

Buck—the inside linebacker aligned on the weakside.

Weak tackle—the defensive tackle who lines up on the weakside (3 technique).

Weak end—the defensive end who lines up on the weakside (7 technique).

Whip—the outside linebacker (strong-safety type of player) who lines up on the weakside (alignment varies).

Weak cornerback—the cornerback who lines up opposite the split end.

STUNT #37

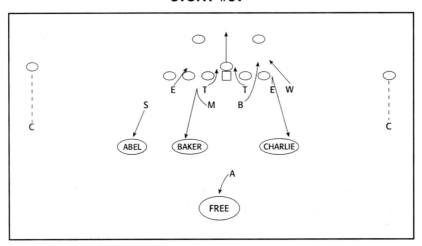

STUNT DESCRIPTION: This **fire zone blitz** sends Buck and Whip and is excellent versus both run and pass.

SECONDARY COVERAGE: Cover 1. The weak end, Mike, and Stud drop into coverage, and the Assassin is free.

STUD: Plays 8 technique versus run. Drops **Abel** versus pass.

STRONG END: Attacks the near shoulder of the offensive tackle. Secures the C gap and contains the quarterback.

STRONG TACKLE: Slants into the A gap.

MIKE: Fakes a blitz toward the B gap. Secures B gap versus run and drops **Baker** versus pass.

BUCK: Blitzes through the B gap.

WEAK TACKLE: Slants into the A gap.

WEAK END: Plays 7 technique versus run. Drops **Charlie** versus pass.

WHIP: Rushes from the edge. Contains the quarterback and weakside run. Chases strongside run.

ASSASSIN: Provides alley support versus run. Free versus pass.

STRONG CORNER: Plays cover 1. Inside/outside technique is dependent upon field position and the distance of the flanker's split.

WEAK CORNER: Plays cover 1. Inside/outside technique is dependent upon field position and the distance of the split end's split.

STUNT #38

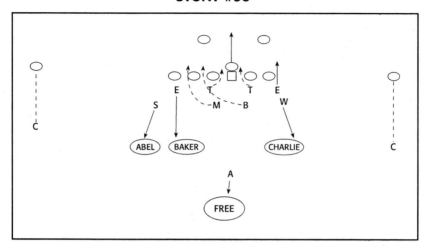

STUNT DESCRIPTION: This **fire zone blitz** sends Mike and Buck on delay blitzes versus pass.

SECONDARY COVERAGE: Cover 1. Both ends and Stud drop into coverage, and the Assassin is free.

STUD: Plays 8 technique versus run. Drops **Abel** versus pass.

STRONG END: Plays 7 technique versus run. Drops **Baker** versus pass.

STRONG TACKLE: Plays 3 technique versus run. Slants into the A gap versus pass.

MIKE: Plays base technique versus run. Blitzes through the outside shoulder of the offensive tackle and contains the quarterback versus pass.

BUCK: Plays base technique versus run. Blitzes through the strongside B gap versus pass.

WEAK TACKLE: Plays 3 technique versus run. Slants into the A gap versus pass.

WEAK END: Plays 7 technique versus run. Contains the quarterback versus pass.

WHIP: Plays 8 technique versus run. Drops **Charlie** versus pass.

ASSASSIN: Provides alley support versus run. Free versus pass.

STRONG CORNER: Plays cover 1. Inside/outside technique is dependent upon field position and the distance of the flanker's split.

WEAK CORNER: Plays cover 1. Inside/outside technique is dependent upon field position and the distance of the split end's split.

STUNT #39

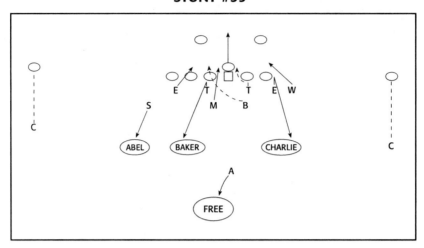

STUNT DESCRIPTION: This **fire zone blitz** sends Mike and Whip. Buck also delay blitzes versus pass.

SECONDARY COVERAGE: Cover 1. Stud, the strong tackle, and the weak end drop into coverage, and the Assassin is free.

STUD: Plays 8 technique versus run. Drops **Abel** versus pass.

STRONG END: Attacks the near shoulder of the offensive tackle. Secures the C gap and contains the quarterback.

STRONG TACKLE: Plays 3 technique versus run. Drops **Baker** versus pass.

MIKE: Blitzes through the A gap.

BUCK: Plays base technique versus run. Blitzes through the strongside B gap versus pass.

WEAK TACKLE: Plays 3 technique versus run. Slants into the A gap versus pass.

WEAK END: Plays 7 technique versus run. Drops **Charlie** versus pass.

WHIP: Rushes from the edge. Contains the quarterback and weakside run. Chases strongside run.

ASSASSIN: Provides alley support versus run. Free versus pass.

STRONG CORNER: Plays cover 1. Inside/outside technique is dependent upon field position and the distance of the flanker's split.

WEAK CORNER: Plays cover 1. Inside/outside technique is dependent upon field position and the distance of the split end's split.

STUNT #40

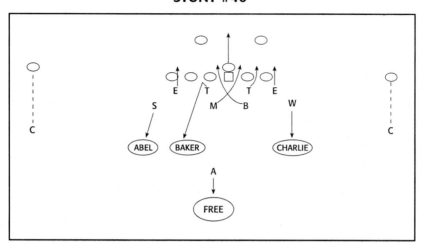

STUNT DESCRIPTION: This **fire zone blitz** sends Mike and Buck and is excellent in passing situations.

SECONDARY COVERAGE: Cover 1. Stud, the strong tackle, and Whip drop into coverage, and the Assassin is free.

STUD: Plays 8 technique versus run. Drops **Abel** versus pass.

STRONG END: Plays 7 technique versus run. Contains the quarterback versus pass.

STRONG TACKLE: Slants to and secures the B gap versus run and drops **Baker** versus pass.

MIKE: Blitzes through the weakside A gap (Buck goes first).

BUCK: Blitzes through the strongside A gap.

WEAK TACKLE: Slants into and controls the B gap.

WEAK END: Plays 7 technique versus run. Contains the quarterback versus pass.

WHIP: Plays 8 technique versus run. Drops **Charlie** versus pass.

ASSASSIN: Provides alley support versus run. Free versus pass.

STRONG CORNER: Plays cover 1. Inside/outside technique is dependent upon field position and the distance of the flanker's split.

WEAK CORNER: Plays cover 1. Inside/outside technique is dependent upon field position and the distance of the split end's split.

STUNT #41

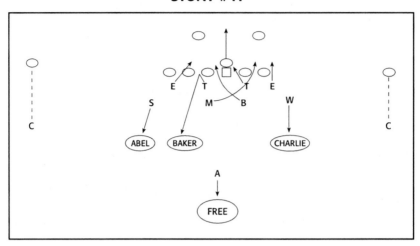

STUNT DESCRIPTION: This **fire zone blitz** sends Mike and Buck and is excellent in passing situations.

SECONDARY COVERAGE: Cover 1. Stud, the strong tackle, and Whip drop into coverage, and the Assassin is free.

STUD: Plays 8 technique versus run. Drops **Abel** versus pass.

STRONG END: Attacks the near shoulder of the offensive tackle. Secures the C gap and contains the quarterback.

STRONG TACKLE: Slants to and secures the B gap versus run and drops **Baker** versus pass.

MIKE: Blitzes through the weakside B gap (Buck goes first).

BUCK: Blitzes through the strongside A gap.

WEAK TACKLE: Slants into and controls the A gap.

WEAK END: Plays 7 technique versus run. Contains the quarterback versus pass.

WHIP: Plays 8 technique versus run. Drops **Charlie** versus pass.

ASSASSIN: Provides alley support versus run. Free versus pass.

STRONG CORNER: Plays cover 1. Inside/outside technique is dependent upon field position and the distance of the flanker's split.

WEAK CORNER: Plays cover 1. Inside/outside technique is dependent upon field position and the distance of the split end's split.

STUNT #42

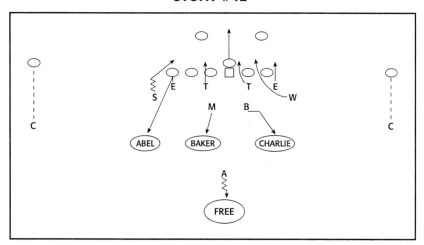

STUNT DESCRIPTION: This **fire zone blitz** has both outside linebackers rushing.

SECONDARY COVERAGE: Cover 1. The strong end, Mike, and Buck drop into coverage, and the Assassin is free.

STUD: Creeps toward the line during cadence and rushes from the edge. Contains the quarterback and strongside run. Chases weakside run.

STRONG END: Plays 7 technique versus run. Drops **Abel** versus pass.

STRONG TACKLE: Plays 3 technique.

MIKE: Plays base technique versus run. Drops **Baker** versus pass.

BUCK: Versus weakside run, scrapes outside and contains. Pursues strongside run from an inside-out position. Drops **Charlie** versus pass.

WEAK TACKLE: Slants across the face of the offensive guard into the A gap.

WEAK END: Plays 7 technique versus run. Contains the quarterback versus pass.

WHIP: Blitzes through the B gap.

ASSASSIN: Provides alley support versus run. Free versus pass.

STRONG CORNER: Plays cover 1. Inside/outside technique is dependent upon field position and the distance of the flanker's split.

WEAK CORNER: Plays cover 1. Inside/outside technique is dependent upon field position and the distance of the split end's split.

STUNT #43

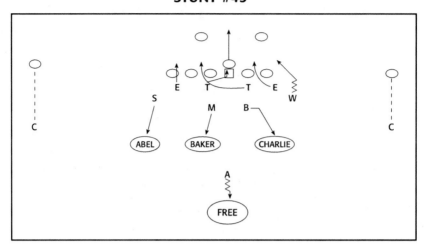

STUNT DESCRIPTION: This **fire zone blitz** has Stud rushing from the edge and incorporates a tackle twist.

SECONDARY COVERAGE: Cover 1. Stud, Mike, and Buck drop into coverage, and the Assassin is free.

STUD: Plays 8 technique versus run. Drops **Abel** versus pass.

STRONG END: Plays 7 technique versus run. Contains the quarterback versus pass.

STRONG TACKLE: Slants into the near shoulder of the center and secures the strongside A gap.

MIKE: Plays base technique versus run. Drops **Baker** versus pass.

BUCK: Pursues strongside and weakside run from an inside-out position. Drops **Charlie** versus pass.

WEAK TACKLE: Loops across the face of the offensive guard and secures the strongside B gap.

WEAK END: Slants across the face of the offensive tackle into the B gap.

WHIP: Rushes from the edge. Contains the quarterback and strongside runs. Chases weakside runs.

ASSASSIN: Provides alley support versus run. Free versus pass.

STRONG CORNER: Plays cover 1. Inside/outside technique is dependent upon field position and the distance of the flanker's split.

WEAK CORNER: Plays cover 1. Inside/outside technique is dependent upon field position and the distance of the split end's split.

STUNT #44

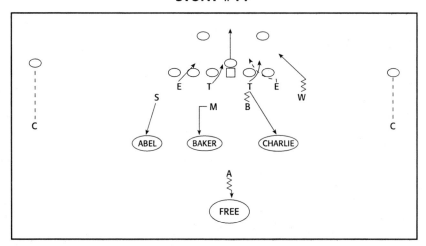

STUNT DESCRIPTION: This **fire zone blitz** has Whip rushing from the edge and features a delayed weakside twin stunt through the B gap.

SECONDARY COVERAGE: Cover 1. Stud, Mike, and Buck drop into coverage, and the Assassin is free.

STUD: Plays 8 technique versus run. Drops **Abel** versus pass.

STRONG END: Slants through the outside shoulder of the offensive tackle. Secures the C gap and contains the quarterback.

STRONG TACKLE: Slants across the face of the offensive guard into the A gap.

MIKE: Secures the B gap versus strongside run. Pursues weakside run from an inside-out position. Drops **Baker** versus pass.

BUCK: Creeps toward the line during cadence and gives the impression that he's blitzing the A gap. Secures the A gap versus run and drops **Charlie** versus pass.

WEAK TACKLE: Slants into the B gap.

WEAK END: Plays 7 technique versus run. Delay rushes through the B gap versus pass.

WHIP: Rushes from the edge. Contains the quarterback and strongside runs. Chases weakside runs.

ASSASSIN: Provides alley support versus run. Free versus pass.

STRONG CORNER: Plays cover 1. Inside/outside technique is dependent upon field position and the distance of the flanker's split.

WEAK CORNER: Plays cover 1. Inside/outside technique is dependent upon field position and the distance of the split end's split.

STUNT #45

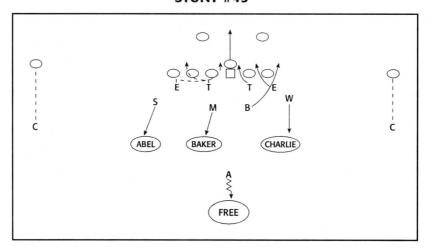

STUNT DESCRIPTION: This **fire zone blitz** features a delayed strongside line twist.

SECONDARY COVERAGE: Cover 1. Stud, Mike, and Whip drop into coverage, and the Assassin is free.

STUD: Plays 8 technique versus run. Drops **Abel** versus pass.

STRONG END: Plays 7 technique versus run. Versus pass, loops across the face of the offensive guard into the strongside A gap. He goes behind the slanting tackle.

STRONG TACKLE: Plays 3 technique versus run. Versus pass, slants across the face of the offensive tackle into the strongside C gap and contains the quarterback.

MIKE: Secures the B gap versus strongside run. Pursues weakside run from an inside-out position. Drops **Baker** versus pass.

BUCK: Blitzes through the outside shoulder of the offensive tackle. Secures the C gap and contains the quarterback.

WEAK TACKLE: Slants into the A gap.

WEAK END: Slants across the face of the offensive tackle into the B gap.

WHIP: Plays 8 technique versus run. Drops **Charlie** versus pass.

ASSASSIN: Provides alley support versus run. Free versus pass.

STRONG CORNER: Plays cover 1. Inside/outside technique is dependent upon field position and the distance of the flanker's split.

WEAK CORNER: Plays cover 1. Inside/outside technique is dependent upon field position and the distance of the split end's split.

STUNT #46

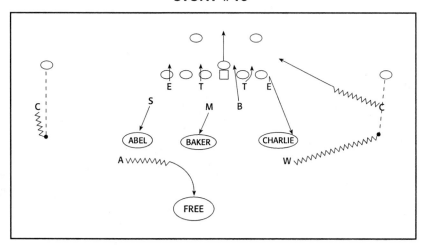

STUNT DESCRIPTION: This **fire zone blitz** features a weakside cornerback blitz.

SECONDARY COVERAGE: Cover 1 disguised as cover 2. Stud, Mike, and the weak end drop off into coverage.

STUD: Plays 8 technique versus run. Drops **Abel** versus pass.

STRONG END: Plays 7 technique versus run. Contains the quarterback versus pass.

STRONG TACKLE: Plays 3 technique.

MIKE: Plays base technique versus run. Drops **Baker** versus pass.

BUCK: Blitzes through the A gap.

WEAK TACKLE: Slants into the B gap.

WEAK END: Plays 7 technique versus run. Drops **Charlie** versus pass.

WHIP: Lines up as though he's playing cover 2. During cadence, moves to a position that enables him to cover the split end (inside technique).

ASSASSIN: Lines up as though he's playing cover 2. Begins moving toward centerfield as Whip begins moving toward the split end. Provides alley support versus run. Free versus pass.

STRONG CORNER: Plays cover 1. Inside/outside technique is dependent upon field position and the flanker's split. Disguises his assignment as though he's playing cover 2.

WEAK CORNER: Disguises his assignment as cover 2. During cadence, slowly creeps inside and blitzes from the edge. Contains the quarterback and weakside runs. Chases strongside runs.

STUNT #47

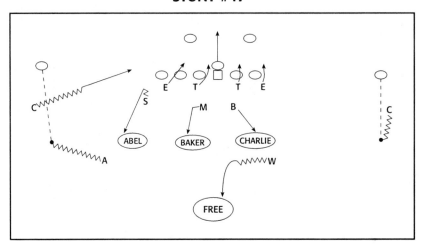

STUNT DESCRIPTION: This **fire zone blitz** features a strongside cornerback blitz.

SECONDARY COVERAGE: Cover 1 disguised as cover 2. Stud, Mike, and Buck drop off into coverage.

STUD: Creeps toward the line during cadence and gives the impression that he intends to rush from the edge. Plays 8 technique versus run. Drops **Abel** versus pass.

STRONG END: Slants through the outside shoulder of the offensive tackle. Secures the C gap and contains the quarterback.

STRONG TACKLE: Slants into the A gap.

MIKE: Fills the B gap versus strongside run. Pursues weakside runs from an inside-out position. Drops **Baker** versus pass.

BUCK: Scrapes outside and contains weakside run. Pursues strongside run from an inside-out position. Drops **Charlie** versus pass.

WEAK TACKLE: Plays 3 technique.

WEAK END: Plays 7 technique versus run. Contains the quarterback versus pass.

WHIP: Lines up as though he's playing cover 2. Begins moving toward centerfield as the Assassin begins moving toward the flanker. Provides alley support versus run. Free versus pass.

ASSASSIN: Lines up as though he's playing cover 2. During cadence, moves to a position that enables him to cover the flanker (inside technique).

STRONG CORNER: Disguises his assignment as cover 2. During cadence, slowly creeps inside and blitzes from the edge. Contains the quarterback and strongside runs. Chases weakside runs.

WEAK CORNER: Plays cover 1. Inside/outside technique is dependent upon field position and the split end's split. Disguises his assignment as though he's playing cover 2.

STUNT #48

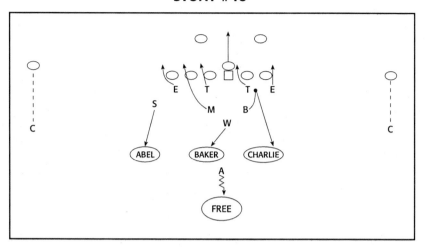

STUNT DESCRIPTION: This **fire zone blitz** provides the defense with excellent strongside run support.

SECONDARY COVERAGE: Cover 1. Stud, Buck, and Whip drop into coverage, and the Assassin is free.

STUD: Plays 8 technique versus run. Drops **Abel** versus pass.

STRONG END: Slants across the face of the tight end. Contains the quarterback and strongside run. Chases weakside run.

STRONG TACKLE: Plays 3 technique.

MIKE: Blitzes through the outside shoulder of the offensive tackle and secures the C gap.

BUCK: Fakes a stunt toward the B gap. Secures the B gap versus run and drops **Charlie** versus pass.

WEAK TACKLE: Slants into the A gap.

WEAK END: Plays 7 technique versus run. Contains the quarterback versus pass.

WHIP: Lines up six yards deep in front of the center. Versus weakside runs, scrapes outside and contains. Checks cutback versus strongside runs. Drops **Baker** versus pass.

ASSASSIN: Provides alley support versus run. Free versus pass.

STRONG CORNER: Plays cover 1. Inside/outside technique is dependent upon field position and the distance of the flanker's split.

WEAK CORNER: Plays cover 1. Inside/outside technique is dependent upon field position and the distance of the split end's split.

STUNT #49

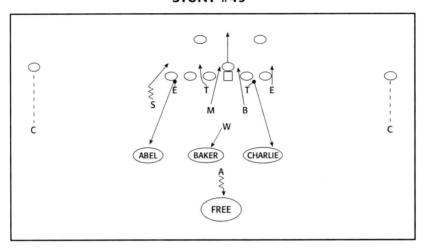

STUNT DESCRIPTION: This **fire zone blitz** is a good run defense in short-yardage situations.

SECONDARY COVERAGE: Cover 1. The strong end, weak tackle, and Whip drop into coverage, and the Assassin is free.

STUD: Creeps toward the line during cadence. Rushes from the edge. Contains the quarterback and strongside run. Chases weakside run.

STRONG END: Plays 7 technique versus run. Drops **Abel** versus pass.

STRONG TACKLE: Slants into the B gap.

MIKE: Blitzes through the A gap.

BUCK: Blitzes through the A gap.

WEAK TACKLE: Slants into and secures the B gap versus run and drops **Charlie** versus pass.

WEAK END: Plays 7 technique versus run. Contains the quarterback versus pass.

WHIP: Lines up six yards deep, directly in front of the center. Versus weakside runs, scrapes outside and contains. Checks cutback versus strongside runs. Drops **Baker** versus pass.

ASSASSIN: Provides alley support versus run. Free versus pass.

STRONG CORNER: Plays cover 1. Inside/outside technique is dependent upon field position and the distance of the flanker's split.

WEAK CORNER: Plays cover 1. Inside/outside technique is dependent upon field position and the distance of the split end's split.

STUNT #50

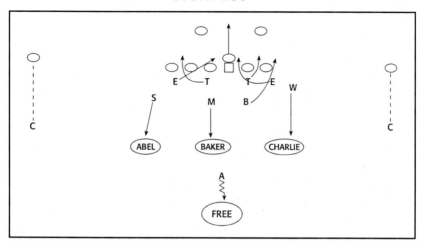

STUNT DESCRIPTION: This **fire zone blitz** provides the defense with excellent weakside run support.

SECONDARY COVERAGE: Cover 1. Stud, Mike, and Whip drop into coverage, and the Assassin is free.

STUD: Plays 8 technique versus run. Drops **Abel** versus pass.

STRONG END: Slants through the outside shoulder of the offensive guard and controls the B gap.

STRONG TACKLE: Loops behind the end. Secures the C gap and contains the quarterback.

MIKE: Plays base technique versus run. Drops **Baker** versus pass.

BUCK: Blitzes through the outside shoulder of the offensive tackle. Secures the C gap versus run and contains the quarterback versus pass.

WEAK TACKLE: Slants into the B gap.

WEAK END: Loops behind the tackle into the weakside A gap.

WHIP: Plays 8 technique versus run. Drops **Charlie** versus pass.

ASSASSIN: Provides alley support versus run. Free versus pass.

STRONG CORNER: Plays cover 1. Inside/outside technique is dependent upon field position and the distance of the flanker's split.

WEAK CORNER: Plays cover 1. Inside/outside technique is dependent upon field position and the distance of the split end's split.

STUNT #51

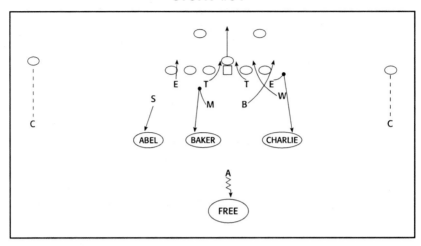

STUNT DESCRIPTION: This **fire zone blitz** gives the initial illusion of a 7-man pass rush.

SECONDARY COVERAGE: Cover 1. Stud, Mike, and the weak end drop into coverage, and the Assassin is free.

STUD: Plays 8 technique versus run. Drops **Abel** versus pass.

STRONG END: Plays 7 technique versus run. Contains the quarterback versus pass.

STRONG TACKLE: Slants into the A gap.

MIKE: Stunts toward and secures the B gap versus run and drops **Baker** versus pass.

BUCK: Blitzes through the outside shoulder of the offensive tackle, contains the quarterback, and secures the C gap versus run.

WEAK TACKLE: Slants into the A gap.

WEAK END: Slants outside. Contains strongside run, chases weakside run, and drops **Charlie** versus pass.

WHIP: Cheats inside slightly and blitzes through the B gap (he goes before Buck).

ASSASSIN: Provides alley support versus run. Free versus pass.

STRONG CORNER: Plays cover 1. Inside/outside technique is dependent upon field position and the distance of the flanker's split.

WEAK CORNER: Plays cover 1. Inside/outside technique is dependent upon field position and the distance of the split end's split.

STUNT #52

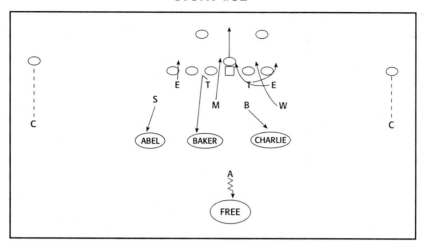

STUNT DESCRIPTION: This **fire zone blitz** gives the initial illusion of a 7-man pass rush and provides the defense with a complex maze of defenders plugging gaps.

SECONDARY COVERAGE: Cover 1. Stud, Buck, and the strong tackle drop into coverage, and the Assassin is free.

STUD: Plays 8 technique versus run. Drops **Abel** versus pass.

STRONG END: Plays 7 technique versus run. Contains the quarterback versus pass.

STRONG TACKLE: Slants to and secures the B gap versus run and drops **Baker** versus pass.

MIKE: Blitzes through the A gap.

BUCK: Versus weakside run, scrapes outside and contains. Pursues strongside run from an inside-out position and drops **Charlie** versus pass.

WEAK TACKLE: Slants across the face of the offensive tackle. Secures the C gap and contains the quarterback.

WEAK END: Loops behind the offensive tackle into the weakside A gap.

WHIP: Blitzes through the B gap. Makes certain that his alignment is deep enough to allow the tackle to clear.

ASSASSIN: Provides alley support versus run. Free versus pass.

STRONG CORNER: Plays cover 1. Inside/outside technique is dependent upon field position and the distance of the flanker's split.

WEAK CORNER: Plays cover 1. Inside/outside technique is dependent upon field position and the distance of the split end's split.

STUNT #53

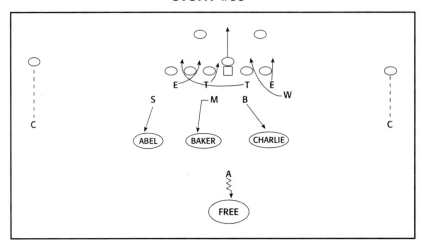

STUNT DESCRIPTION: This **fire zone blitz** sends Whip and provides the defense with a line twist.

SECONDARY COVERAGE: Cover 1. Stud, Mike, and Buck drop into coverage, and the Assassin is free.

STUD: Plays 8 technique versus run. Drops **Abel** versus pass.

STRONG END: Slants across the face of the offensive tackle into the B gap.

STRONG TACKLE: Slants into the A gap.

MIKE: Shuffles slightly to the outside at the snap. Versus strongside run, scrapes into the C gap. Pursues weakside run from an inside-out position. Versus pass, drops **Baker**.

BUCK: Versus weakside run, scrapes outside and contains. Pursues strongside run from an inside-out position, and drops **Charlie** versus pass.

WEAK TACKLE: Slants across the face of the offensive tackle into the strongside C gap. Secures C gap versus run and contains the quarterback versus pass.

WEAK END: Plays 7 technique versus run. Contains the quarterback versus pass.

WHIP: Blitzes through the B gap.

ASSASSIN: Provides alley support versus run. Free versus pass.

STRONG CORNER: Plays cover 1. Inside/outside technique is dependent upon field position and the distance of the flanker's split.

WEAK CORNER: Plays cover 1. Inside/outside technique is dependent upon field position and the distance of the split end's split.

STUNT #54

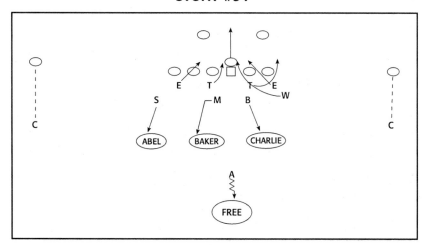

STUNT DESCRIPTION: This **fire zone blitz** provides the defense with a weakside line twist.

SECONDARY COVERAGE: Cover 1. Stud, Mike, and Buck drop into coverage, and the Assassin is free.

STUD: Plays 8 technique versus run. Drops **Abel** versus pass.

STRONG END: Slants through the outside shoulder of the offensive tackle. Secures the C gap and contains the quarterback.

STRONG TACKLE: Slants into the A gap.

MIKE: Plays base technique versus run. Drops **Baker** versus pass.

BUCK: Versus weakside run, scrapes outside and contains. Pursues strongside run from an inside-out position, and drops **Charlie** versus pass.

WEAK TACKLE: Loops behind the end, secures the C gap, and contains the quarterback.

WEAK END: Slants across the face of the offensive tackle into the B gap.

WHIP: Blitzes through the A gap.

ASSASSIN: Provides alley support versus run. Free versus pass.

STRONG CORNER: Plays cover 1. Inside/outside technique is dependent upon field position and the distance of the flanker's split.

WEAK CORNER: Plays cover 1. Inside/outside technique is dependent upon field position and the distance of the split end's split.

STUNT #55

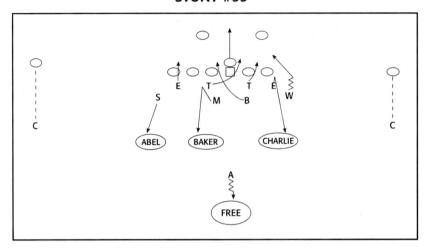

STUNT DESCRIPTION: This **fire zone blitz** provides the defense with the initial illusion of a 7-man pass rush.

SECONDARY COVERAGE: Cover 1. Stud, Mike, and the weak end drop into coverage, and the Assassin is free.

STUD: Plays 8 technique versus run. Drops **Abel** versus pass.

STRONG END: Plays 7 technique versus run. Contains the quarterback versus pass.

STRONG TACKLE: Slants across the face of the center into the weakside A gap.

MIKE: Fakes a blitz toward the B gap and secures B gap versus run. Drops **Baker** versus pass.

BUCK: Blitzes through the strongside A gap.

WEAK TACKLE: Slants into the B gap.

WEAK END: Plays 7 technique versus run. Drops **Charlie** versus pass.

WHIP: Creeps toward the line during cadence and rushes from the edge. Contains the quarterback and weakside run. Chases strongside run.

ASSASSIN: Provides alley support versus run. Free versus pass.

STRONG CORNER: Plays cover 1. Inside/outside technique is dependent upon field position and the distance of the flanker's split.

WEAK CORNER: Plays cover 1. Inside/outside technique is dependent upon field position and the distance of the split end's split.

CHAPTER 7

COLLEGE AND PRO 4-3 FIRE ZONE BLITZES

Strong cornerback—the cornerback who lines up opposite the flanker.

Strong safety—the safety who lines up toward the tight-end side.

Free safety—the safety who lines up toward the split-end side.

Stud—the outside linebacker who lines up on the strongside.

Strong end—the defensive end who lines up on the strongside.

Strong tackle—the defensive tackle who lines up on the strongside.

Mike—the middle linebacker.

Weak tackle—the defensive tackle who lines up on the weakside.

Weak end—the defensive end who lines up on the weakside.

Whip—the outside linebacker who lines up on the weakside.

Weak cornerback—the cornerback who lines up opposite the split end.

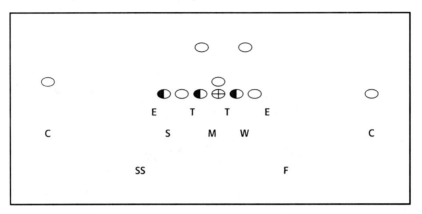

Figure 7-1a. College 4-3

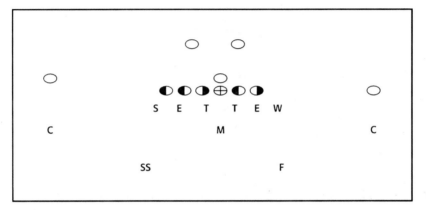

Figure 7-1b. Pro 4-3

STUNT #56

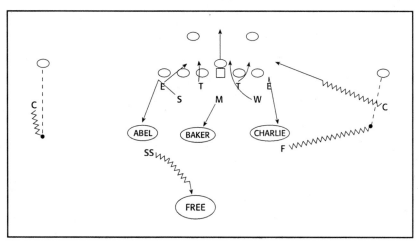

STUNT DESCRIPTION: This college 4-3 **fire zone blitz** features a weakside cornerback blitz.

SECONDARY COVERAGE: Cover 1 disguised as cover 2. Mike, Stud, and the weak end drop into coverage, and the strong safety is free.

STRONG SAFETY: Lines up as though he's playing cover 2. During cadence, moves toward the deep middle. Provides alley support versus run and plays centerfield versus pass.

STUD: Stunts toward the outside shoulder of the tight end. Contains strongside run, chases weakside run, and drops **Abel** versus pass.

STRONG END: Slants through the outside shoulder of the offensive tackle. Secures the C gap and contains the quarterback.

STRONG TACKLE: Plays 3 technique.

MIKE: Plays base technique versus run. Drops **Baker** versus pass.

WEAK TACKLE: Slants into the B gap.

WEAK END: Plays 7 technique versus run. Drops **Charlie** versus pass.

WHIP: Blitzes through the weakside A gap.

FREE SAFETY: Lines up as though he's playing cover 2. During cadence, moves to a position that enables him to cover the split end.

STRONG CORNER: Plays cover 1. Inside/outside technique is dependent upon field position and the distance of the flanker's split. Disguises his assignment as though he's playing cover 2.

WEAK CORNER: Creeps inside during cadence and blitzes from the edge. Contains the quarterback and weakside run. Chases strongside run.

STUNT #57

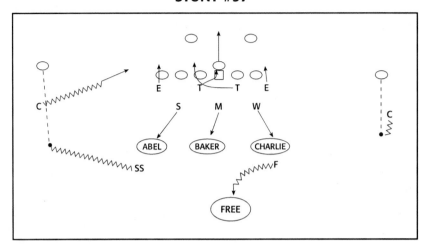

STUNT DESCRIPTION: This college 4-3 **fire zone blitz** features a strongside cornerback blitz.

SECONDARY COVERAGE: Cover 1 disguised as cover 2. Mike, Stud, and Whip drop into coverage, and the free safety plays centerfield.

STRONG SAFETY: Lines up as though he's playing cover 2. During cadence, moves to a position that enables him to cover the flanker.

STUD: Plays base technique versus run. Drops **Abel** versus pass.

STRONG END: Plays 9 technique.

STRONG TACKLE: Slants into the near shoulder of the center and controls the strongside A gap.

MIKE: Plays base technique versus run. Drops **Baker** versus pass.

WEAK TACKLE: Slants through the outside shoulder of the offensive guard and secures the strongside B gap.

WEAK END: Plays 7 technique versus run. Contains the quarterback versus pass.

WHIP: Plays base technique versus run. Drops **Charlie** versus pass.

FREE SAFETY: Lines up as though he's playing cover 2. During cadence, moves toward the deep middle. Provides alley support versus run and plays centerfield versus pass.

STRONG CORNER: Creeps inside during cadence and blitzes from the edge. Contains the quarterback and strongside run. Chases weakside run.

WEAK CORNER: Plays cover 1. Inside/outside technique dependent upon field position and the distance of the split end's split. Disguises his assignment as though he's playing cover 2.

STUNT #58

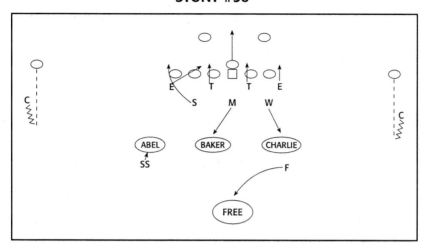

STUNT DESCRIPTION: This college 4-3 **fire zone blitz** sends Stud.

SECONDARY COVERAGE: Cover 1 disguised as cover 2. The strong safety, Mike, and Whip drop into coverage, and the free safety plays centerfield.

STRONG SAFETY: Lines up as though he's playing cover 2. Contains strongside run and provides alley support to weakside run. Drops **Abel** versus pass.

STUD: Stunts through the outside shoulder of the tight end. Secures the D gap and contains the quarterback.

STRONG END: Slants through the near shoulder of the offensive tackle and controls the C gap.

STRONG TACKLE: Plays 3 technique.

MIKE: Plays base technique versus run. Drops **Baker** versus pass.

WEAK TACKLE: Plays 1 technique.

WEAK END: Plays 7 technique versus run. Contains the quarterback versus pass.

WHIP: Plays base technique versus run. Drops **Charlie** versus pass.

FREE SAFETY: Lines up as though he's playing cover 2. Contains weakside run and provides alley support to strongside run. Drops to centerfield versus pass.

STRONG CORNER: Plays cover 1. Inside/outside technique dependent upon field position and the distance of the flanker's split. Disguises his assignment as though he's playing cover 2.

WEAK CORNER: Plays cover 1. Inside/outside technique dependent upon field position and the distance of the split end's split. Disguises his assignment as though he's playing cover 2.

STUNT #59

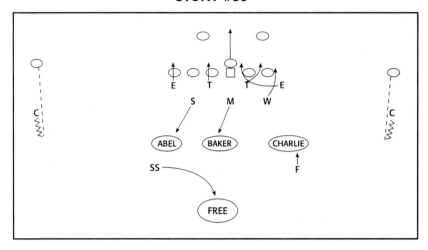

STUNT DESCRIPTION: This college 4-3 **fire zone blitz** sends Whip and provides the defense with a weakside line twist.

SECONDARY COVERAGE: Cover 1 disguised as cover 2. The free safety, Mike, and Stud drop into coverage, and the strong safety plays centerfield.

STRONG SAFETY: Lines up as though he's playing cover 2. Contains strongside run and provides alley support to weakside run. Plays centerfield versus pass.

STUD: Plays base technique versus run. Drops **Abel** versus pass.

STRONG END: Plays 9 technique versus run. Contains the quarterback versus pass.

STRONG TACKLE: Plays 3 technique.

MIKE: Plays base technique versus run. Drops **Baker** versus pass.

WEAK TACKLE: Lines up in a 2 technique and slants into the B gap.

WEAK END: Loops behind the tackle into the weakside A gap.

WHIP: Stunts through the outside shoulder of the offensive tackle. Secures the C gap and contains the quarterback.

FREE SAFETY: Lines up as though he's playing cover 2. Contains weakside run and provides alley support to strongside run. Drops **Charlie** versus pass.

STRONG CORNER: Plays cover 1. Inside/outside technique dependent upon field position and the distance of the flanker's split. Disguises his assignment as though he's playing cover 2.

WEAK CORNER: Plays cover 1. Inside/outside technique dependent upon field position and the distance of the split end's split. Disguises his assignment as though he's playing cover 2.

STUNT #60

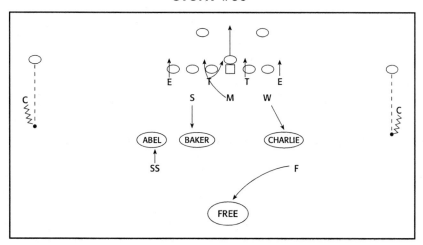

STUNT DESCRIPTION: This college 4-3 **fire zone blitz** sends Mike.

SECONDARY COVERAGE: Cover 1 disguised as cover 2. The strong safety, Stud, and Whip drop into coverage, and the free safety plays centerfield.

STRONG SAFETY: Lines up as though he's playing cover 2. Contains strongside run and provides alley support to weakside run. Drops **Abel** versus pass.

STUD: Plays base technique versus run. Drops **Baker** versus pass.

STRONG END: Plays 9 technique versus run. Contains the quarterback versus pass.

STRONG TACKLE: Slants across the face of the offensive guard into the A gap.

MIKE: Blitzes through the B gap.

WEAK TACKLE: Plays 1 technique.

WEAK END: Plays 7 technique versus run. Contains the quarterback versus pass.

WHIP: Plays base technique versus run. Drops **Charlie** versus pass.

FREE SAFETY: Lines up as though he's playing cover 2. Contains weakside run and provides alley support to strongside run. Drops to centerfield versus pass.

STRONG CORNER: Plays cover 1. Inside/outside technique dependent upon field position and the distance of the flanker's split. Disguises his assignment as though he's playing cover 2.

WEAK CORNER: Plays cover 1. Inside/outside technique dependent upon field position and the distance of the split end's split. Disguises his assignment as though he's playing cover 2.

STUNT #61

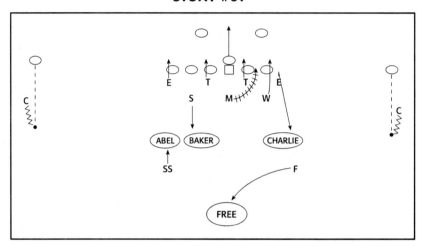

STUNT DESCRIPTION: This college 4-3 **fire zone blitz** sends Whip and provides the defense with a delayed blitz by Mike versus pass.

SECONDARY COVERAGE: Cover 1 disguised as cover 2. The strong safety, Stud, and the weak end drop into coverage, and the free safety plays centerfield.

STRONG SAFETY: Lines up as though he's playing cover 2. Contains strongside run and provides alley support to weakside run. Drops **Abel** versus pass.

STUD: Plays base technique versus run. Drops **Baker** versus pass.

STRONG END: Plays 9 technique versus run. Contains the quarterback versus pass.

STRONG TACKLE: Plays 3 technique.

MIKE: Plays base technique versus run. Delay blitzes through the weakside B gap versus pass.

WEAK TACKLE: Plays 1 technique.

WEAK END: Plays 7 technique versus run. Drops **Charlie** versus pass.

WHIP: Blitzes through the outside shoulder of the offensive tackle. Secures the C gap versus run and contains the quarterback versus pass.

FREE SAFETY: Lines up as though he's playing cover 2. Contains weakside run and provides alley support to strongside run. Drops to centerfield versus pass.

STRONG CORNER: Plays cover 1. Inside/outside technique dependent upon field position and the distance of the flanker's split. Disguises his assignment as though he's playing cover 2.

WEAK CORNER: Plays cover 1. Inside/outside technique dependent upon field position and the distance of the split end's split. Disguises his assignment as though he's playing cover 2.

STUNT #62

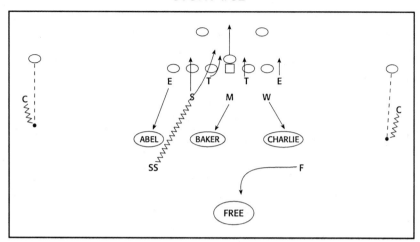

STUNT DESCRIPTION: This college 4-3 **fire zone blitz** sends Stud and provides the defense with a strong safety blitz.

SECONDARY COVERAGE: Cover 1 disguised as cover 2. The strong end, Mike, and Whip drop into coverage, and the free safety plays centerfield.

STRONG SAFETY: Lines up as though he's playing cover 2. Creeps toward the line during cadence and blitzes through the B gap at the snap of the ball.

STUD: Blitzes through the outside shoulder of the offensive tackle. Secures the C gap and contains the quarterback.

STRONG END: Plays 9 technique versus run. Drops **Abel** versus pass.

STRONG TACKLE: Slants into the A gap.

MIKE: Plays base technique versus run. Drops **Baker** versus pass.

WEAK TACKLE: Plays 1 technique.

WEAK END: Plays 7 technique versus run. Contains the quarterback versus pass.

WHIP: Plays base technique versus run. Drops Charlie versus pass.

FREE SAFETY: Lines up as though he's playing cover 2. Begins moving toward centerfield during cadence. Provides alley support for run. Drops deep middle versus pass.

STRONG CORNER: Plays cover 1. Inside/outside technique dependent upon field position and the distance of the flanker's split. Disguises his assignment as though he's playing cover 2.

WEAK CORNER: Plays cover 1. Inside/outside technique dependent upon field position and the distance of the split end's split. Disguises his assignment as though he's playing cover 2.

STUNT #63

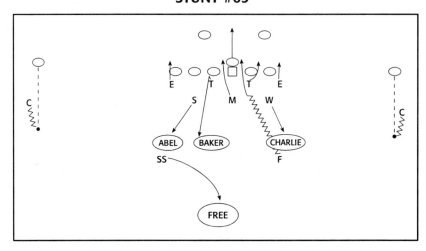

STUNT DESCRIPTION: This college 4-3 **fire zone blitz** sends Mike and provides the defense with a free safety blitz.

SECONDARY COVERAGE: Cover 1 disguised as cover 2. Stud, the strong tackle, and Whip drop into coverage, and the strong safety plays centerfield.

STRONG SAFETY: Lines up as though he's playing cover 2. Begins moving toward centerfield during cadence. Provides alley support for run. Drops deep middle versus pass.

STUD: Plays base technique versus run. Drops **Abel** versus pass.

STRONG END: Plays 9 technique versus run. Contains the quarterback versus pass.

STRONG TACKLE: Plays 3 technique versus run. Drops **Baker** versus pass.

MIKE: Blitzes through the strongside A gap.

WEAK TACKLE: Cheats to a 2 technique and slants into the B gap.

WEAK END: Plays 7 technique versus run. Contains the quarterback versus pass.

WHIP: Plays base technique versus run. Drops **Charlie** versus pass.

FREE SAFETY: Lines up as though he's playing cover 2. Creeps toward the line during cadence and blitzes through the weakside A gap at the snap of the ball.

STRONG CORNER: Plays cover 1. Inside/outside technique dependent upon field position and the distance of the flanker's split. Disguises his assignment as though he's playing cover 2.

WEAK CORNER: Plays cover 1. Inside/outside technique dependent upon field position and the distance of the split end's split. Disguises his assignment as though he's playing cover 2.

STUNT #64

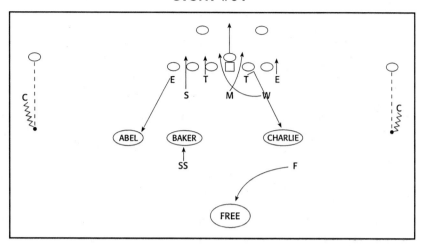

STUNT DESCRIPTION: This college 4-3 **fire zone blitz** sends Mike, Stud, and Whip.

SECONDARY COVERAGE: Cover 1 disguised as cover 2. The strong end, strong safety, and the weak tackle drop into coverage, and the free safety plays centerfield.

STRONG SAFETY: Lines up as though he's playing cover 2. Contains strongside run and provides alley support to weakside run. Drops **Abel** versus pass.

STUD: Blitzes through the outside shoulder of the offensive tackle. Secures the C gap and contains the quarterback.

STRONG END: Plays 9 technique versus run. Drops **Baker** versus pass.

STRONG TACKLE: Plays 3 technique.

MIKE: Blitzes through the weakside A gap.

WEAK TACKLE: Cheats to a 2 technique. Slants into and secures the B gap versus run, and drops **Charlie** versus pass.

WEAK END: Plays 7 technique versus run. Contains the quarterback versus pass.

WHIP: Blitzes through the strongside A gap.

FREE SAFETY: Lines up as though he's playing cover 2. Contains weakside run and provides alley support to strongside run. Drops to centerfield versus pass.

STRONG CORNER: Plays cover 1. Inside/outside technique dependent upon field position and the distance of the flanker's split. Disguises his assignment as though he's playing cover 2.

WEAK CORNER: Plays cover 1. Inside/outside technique dependent upon field position and the distance of the split end's split. Disguises his assignment as though he's playing cover 2.

STUNT #65

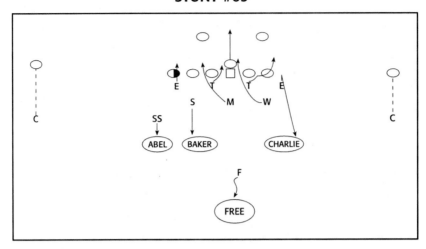

STUNT DESCRIPTION: This college 4-3 **fire zone blitz** sends Mike and Whip.

SECONDARY COVERAGE: Cover 1 disguised as cover 3. The strong safety, Stud, and the weak end drop into coverage, and the free safety plays centerfield.

STRONG SAFETY: Lines up as though he's playing cover 3 sky. Contains strongside run and drops **Abel** versus pass.

STUD: Scrapes outside versus strongside run, pursues weakside run from an inside-out position, and drops **Baker** versus pass.

STRONG END: Plays 7 technique versus run. Contains the quarterback versus pass.

STRONG TACKLE: Slants into the A gap.

MIKE: Blitzes through the strongside B gap.

WEAK TACKLE: Cheats to a 2 technique. Slants into and secures the B gap versus run, and contain rushes versus pass.

WEAK END: Plays 7 technique versus run. Drops **Charlie** versus pass.

WHIP: Blitzes through the strongside A gap.

FREE SAFETY: Lines up as though he's playing cover 3. Provides alley support versus run. Plays centerfield versus pass.

STRONG CORNER: Plays cover 1. Inside/outside technique is dependent upon field position and the distance of the flanker's split.

WEAK CORNER: Plays cover 1. Inside/outside technique is dependent upon field position and the distance of the split end's split.

STUNT #66

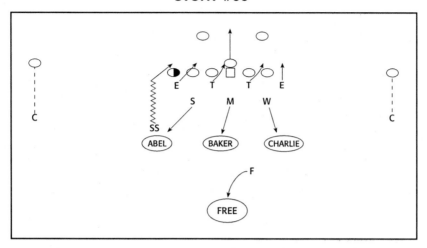

STUNT DESCRIPTION: This college 4-3 **fire zone blitz** sends the strong safety and provides the defense with a weakside line slant.

SECONDARY COVERAGE: Cover 1 disguised as cover 3. All three linebackers drop into coverage, and the free safety plays centerfield.

STRONG SAFETY: Lines up as though he's playing cover 3 sky. Creeps toward the line during cadence and rushes from the edge. Contains the quarterback and strongside run. Chases weakside run.

STUD: Versus strongside run, scrapes outside and helps contain. Pursues weakside run from an inside-out position, and drops **Abel** versus pass.

STRONG END: Lines up in a 7 technique, slants through the offensive tackle's near shoulder at the snap and secures the C gap.

STRONG TACKLE: Slants into the A gap.

MIKE: Secures the B gap versus strongside run and the A gap versus weakside run. Drops **Baker** versus pass.

WEAK TACKLE: Cheats to a 2 technique. Slants into and secures the B gap.

WEAK END: Plays 7 technique versus run. Contains the quarterback versus pass.

WHIP: Plays base technique versus run. Drops **Charlie** versus pass.

FREE SAFETY: Lines up as though he's playing cover 3. Provides alley support versus run. Plays centerfield versus pass.

STRONG CORNER: Plays cover 1. Inside/outside technique is dependent upon field position and the distance of the flanker's split.

WEAK CORNER: Plays cover 1. Inside/outside technique is dependent upon field position and the distance of the split end's split.

STUNT #67

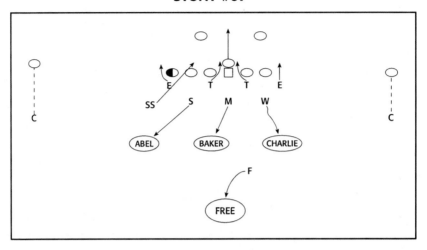

STUNT DESCRIPTION: This college 4-3 **fire zone blitz** sends the strong safety on an inside blitz.

SECONDARY COVERAGE: Cover 1 disguised as cover 3. All three linebackers drop into coverage, and the free safety plays centerfield.

STRONG SAFETY: Lines up as though he's playing cover 3 sky. Blitzes through the near shoulder of the offensive tackle and secures the C gap.

STUD: Pursues strongside and weakside run from an inside-out position. Drops **Abel** versus pass.

STRONG END: Lines up in a 9 technique and slants outside at the snap. Contains the quarterback and strongside run. Chases weakside run.

STRONG TACKLE: Slants into the A gap.

MIKE: Secures both B gaps versus run. Drops **Baker** versus pass.

WEAK TACKLE: Slants into the A gap.

WEAK END: Plays 7 technique versus run. Contains the quarterback versus pass.

WHIP: Plays base technique versus run. Drops **Charlie** versus pass.

FREE SAFETY: Lines up as though he's playing cover 3. Provides alley support versus run. Plays centerfield versus pass.

STRONG CORNER: Plays cover 1. Inside/outside technique is dependent upon field position and the distance of the flanker's split.

WEAK CORNER: Plays cover 1. Inside/outside technique dependent upon field position and the distance of the split end's split.

STUNT #68

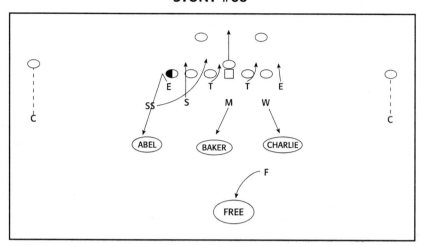

STUNT DESCRIPTION: This college 4-3 **fire zone blitz** sends Stud and provides the defense with a strong safety blitz.

SECONDARY COVERAGE: Cover 1 disguised as cover 3. The strong end, Mike, and Whip drop into coverage, and the free safety plays centerfield.

STRONG SAFETY: Lines up as though he's playing cover 3 sky. Blitzes through the B gap.

STUD: Blitzes through the outside shoulder of the offensive tackle. Secures the C gap and contains the quarterback.

STRONG END: Lines up in a 9 technique and slants outside at the snap. Contains strongside run and chases weakside run. Drops **Abel** versus pass.

STRONG TACKLE: Slants into the A gap.

MIKE: Pursues strongside and weakside run from an inside-out position. Drops **Baker** versus pass.

WEAK TACKLE: Cheats to a 2 technique and slants into the B gap.

WEAK END: Plays 7 technique versus run. Contains the quarterback versus pass.

WHIP: Plays base technique versus run. Drops **Charlie** versus pass.

FREE SAFETY: Lines up as though he's playing cover 3. Provides alley support versus run. Plays centerfield versus pass.

STRONG CORNER: Plays cover 1. Inside/outside technique is dependent upon field position and the distance of the flanker's split.

WEAK CORNER: Plays cover 1. Inside/outside technique is dependent upon field position and the distance of the split end's split.

STUNT #69

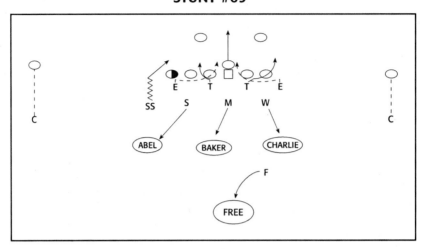

STUNT DESCRIPTION: This college 4-3 **fire zone blitz** features a strong safety blitz and a delayed line twist.

SECONDARY COVERAGE: Cover 1 disguised as cover 3. Stud, Mike, and Whip drop into coverage, and the free safety plays centerfield.

STRONG SAFETY: Lines up as though he's playing cover 3 sky. Rushes from the edge at the snap. Contains the quarterback and strongside run. Chases weakside run.

STUD: Versus strongside run, scrapes outside and helps contain. Pursues weakside run from an inside-out position. Drops **Abel** versus pass.

STRONG END: Plays 7 technique versus run. Versus pass, loops through the strongside A gap.

STRONG TACKLE: Plays 3 technique. Versus pass, he must gain quick penetration through the B gap.

MIKE: Plays base technique versus run. Drops **Baker** versus pass.

WEAK TACKLE: Cheats to a 2 technique, and slants into and controls the B gap versus run. Contain rushes versus pass.

WEAK END: Plays 7 technique versus run. Versus pass, loops through the strongside A gap.

WHIP: Plays base technique versus run. Drops **Charlie** versus pass.

FREE SAFETY: Lines up as though he's playing cover 3. Provides alley support versus run. Plays centerfield versus pass.

STRONG CORNER: Plays cover 1. Inside/outside technique is dependent upon field position and the distance of the flanker's split.

WEAK CORNER: Plays cover 1. Inside/outside technique is dependent upon field position and the distance of the split end's split.

STUNT #70

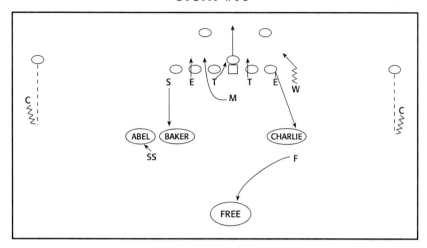

STUNT DESCRIPTION: This pro 4-3 **fire zone blitz** sends Mike and Whip.

SECONDARY COVERAGE: Cover 1 disguised as cover 2. The strong safety, Stud, and the weak end drop into coverage, and the free safety plays centerfield.

STRONG SAFETY: Lines up as though he's playing cover 2. Contains strongside run and provides alley support to weakside run. Drops **Abel** versus pass.

STUD: Plays 9 technique versus run. Drops **Baker** versus pass.

STRONG END: Plays 5 technique versus run. Contains the quarterback versus pass.

STRONG TACKLE: Lines up in a 1 technique and slants into the A gap.

MIKE: Blitzes through the B gap.

WEAK TACKLE: Plays 1 technique.

WEAK END: Plays 5 technique versus run. Drops **Charlie** versus pass.

WHIP: Rushes from the edge. Contains the quarterback and weakside run. Chases strongside run.

FREE SAFETY: Lines up as though he's playing cover 2. Helps contain weakside run and provides alley support versus strongside run. Drops to centerfield versus pass.

STRONG CORNER: Plays cover 1. Inside/outside technique is dependent upon field position and the distance of the flanker's split. Disguises his assignment as though he's playing cover 2.

WEAK CORNER: Plays cover 1. Inside/outside technique is dependent upon field position and the distance of the split end's split. Disguises his assignment as though he's playing cover 2.

STUNT #71

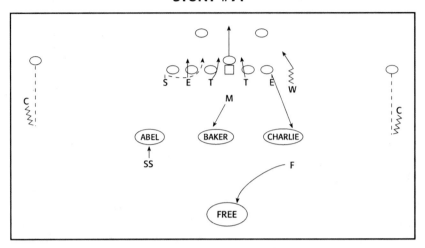

STUNT DESCRIPTION: This pro 4-3 **fire zone blitz** sends Whip and then Stud (on a delay rush versus pass).

SECONDARY COVERAGE: Cover 1 disguised as cover 2. The strong safety, Mike and the weak end drop into coverage, and the free safety plays centerfield.

STRONG SAFETY: Lines up as though he's playing cover 2. Helps contain strongside run and provides alley support versus weakside run. Drops **Abel** versus pass.

STUD: Plays 9 technique versus run. Delay rushes through the strongside B gap versus pass.

STRONG END: Plays 5 technique versus run. Contains the quarterback versus pass.

STRONG TACKLE: Plays 1 technique.

MIKE: Controls both B gaps versus run. Drops **Baker** versus pass.

WEAK TACKLE: Plays 1 technique.

WEAK END: Plays 5 technique versus run. Drops **Charlie** versus pass.

WHIP: Rushes from the edge. Contains the quarterback and weakside run. Chases strongside run.

FREE SAFETY: Lines up as though he's playing cover 2. Helps contain weakside run and provides alley support versus strongside run. Drops to centerfield versus pass.

STRONG CORNER: Plays cover 1. Inside/outside technique is dependent upon field position and the distance of the flanker's split. Disguises his assignment as though he's playing cover 2.

WEAK CORNER: Plays cover 1. Inside/outside technique is dependent upon field position and the distance of the split end's split. Disguises his assignment as though he's playing cover 2.

STUNT #72

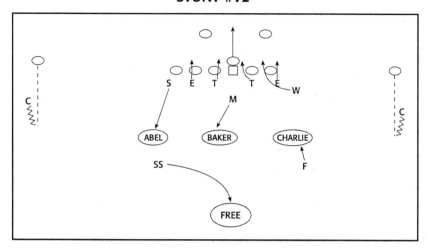

STUNT DESCRIPTION: This pro 4-3 **fire zone blitz** sends Whip.

SECONDARY COVERAGE: Cover 1 disguised as cover 2. The free safety, Mike, and Stud drop into coverage, and the strong safety plays centerfield.

STRONG SAFETY: Lines up as though he's playing cover 2. Contains strongside run and provides alley support versus weakside run. Drops centerfield versus pass.

STUD: Plays 9 technique versus run. Drops **Abel** versus pass.

STRONG END: Plays 5 technique versus run. Contains the quarterback versus pass.

STRONG TACKLE: Plays 1 technique.

MIKE: Controls both B gaps versus run. Drops **Baker** versus pass.

WEAK TACKLE: Lines up in a 1 technique and slants into the A gap.

WEAK END: Plays 5 technique versus run. Contains the quarterback versus pass.

WHIP: Blitzes through the weakside B gap.

FREE SAFETY: Lines up as though he's playing cover 2. Contains weakside run and provides alley support versus strongside run. Drops **Charlie** versus pass.

STRONG CORNER: Plays cover 1. Inside/outside technique is dependent upon field position and the distance of the flanker's split. Disguises his assignment as though he's playing cover 2.

WEAK CORNER: Plays cover 1. Inside/outside technique is dependent upon field position and the distance of the split end's split. Disguises his assignment as though he's playing cover 2.

STUNT #73

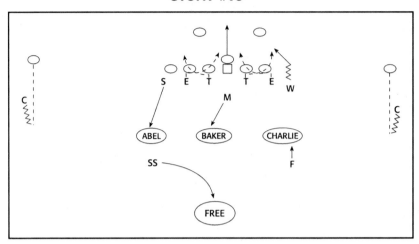

STUNT DESCRIPTION: This pro 4-3 **fire zone blitz** sends Whip and provides the defense with a delayed line twist.

SECONDARY COVERAGE: Cover 1 disguised as cover 2. The free safety, Mike, and Stud drop into coverage, and the strong safety plays centerfield.

STRONG SAFETY: Lines up as though he's playing cover 2. Contains strongside run and provides alley support versus weakside run. Drops centerfield versus pass.

STUD: Plays 9 technique versus run. Drops **Abel** versus pass.

STRONG END: Plays 5 technique versus run. Engages the tackle's block, gains penetration, and then loops behind the tackle into the A gap versus pass.

STRONG TACKLE: Lines up in a 2 technique and secures the B gap versus run. Contain rushes versus pass.

MIKE: Controls both A gaps versus run. Drops **Baker** versus pass.

WEAK TACKLE: Lines up in a 2 technique and secures the B gap versus run. Contain rushes versus pass.

WEAK END: Plays 5 technique versus run. Engages the tackle's block, gains penetration, and then loops behind the tackle into the A gap versus pass.

WHIP: Rushes from edge. Contains the quarterback and weakside run. Chases strongside run.

FREE SAFETY: Lines up as though he's playing cover 2. Contains weakside run and provides alley support versus strongside run. Drops **Charlie** versus pass.

STRONG CORNER: Plays cover 1. Inside/outside technique is dependent upon field position and the distance of the flanker's split. Disguises his assignment as though he's playing cover 2.

WEAK CORNER: Plays cover 1. Inside/outside technique is dependent upon field position and the distance of the split end's split. Disguises his assignment as though he's playing cover 2.

STUNT #74

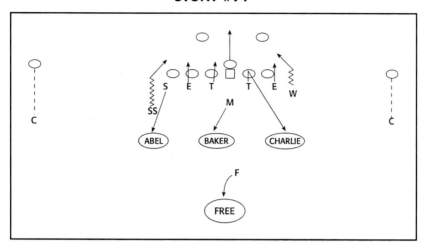

STUNT DESCRIPTION: This pro 4-3 **fire zone blitz** sends Whip and features a strong safety blitz.

SECONDARY COVERAGE: Cover 1 disguised as cover 3. Stud, Mike, and the weak tackle drop into coverage, and the free safety plays centerfield.

STRONG SAFETY: Lines up as though he's playing cover 3 sky. Creeps toward the line during cadence and rushes from the edge at the snap. Contains the quarterback and strongside run. Chases weakside run.

STUD: Plays 9 technique versus run. Drops **Abel** versus pass.

STRONG END: Plays 5 technique.

STRONG TACKLE: Plays 1 technique.

MIKE: Controls the strongside B gap and the weakside A gap versus run. Drops **Baker** versus pass.

WEAK TACKLE: Plays 2 technique versus run. Drops **Charlie** versus pass.

WEAK END: Plays 5 technique.

WHIP: Rushes from the edge. Contains the quarterback and weakside run. Chases strongside run.

FREE SAFETY: Lines up as though he's playing cover 3. Provides alley support versus run. Plays centerfield versus pass.

STRONG CORNER: Plays cover 1. Inside/outside technique is dependent upon field position and the distance of the flanker's split.

WEAK CORNER: Plays cover 1. Inside/outside technique is dependent upon field position and the distance of the split end's split.

STUNT #75

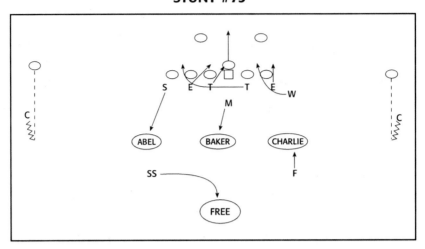

STUNT DESCRIPTION: This pro 4-3 **fire zone blitz** sends Whip and provides the defense with a line twist.

SECONDARY COVERAGE: Cover 1 disguised as cover 2. The free safety, Mike, and Stud will drop into coverage, and the strong safety plays centerfield.

STRONG SAFETY: Lines up as though he's playing cover 2. Contains strongside run and provides alley support versus weakside run. Plays centerfield versus pass.

STUD: Plays 9 technique versus run. Drops **Abel** versus pass.

STRONG END: Slants across the face of the offensive tackle into the B gap.

STRONG TACKLE: Slants across the face of the offensive guard into the A gap.

MIKE: Pursues strongside and weakside run from an inside-out position. Drops **Baker** versus pass.

WEAK TACKLE: Loops across the face of the offensive tackle into the strongside C gap. Secures the C gap versus run and contains the quarterback.

WEAK END: Plays 5 technique versus run. Contains the quarterback versus pass.

WHIP: Blitzes through the B gap.

FREE SAFETY: Lines up as though he's playing cover 2. Contains weakside run and provides alley support versus strongside run. Drops **Charlie** versus pass.

STRONG CORNER: Plays cover 1. Inside/outside technique is dependent upon field position and the distance of the flanker's split. Disguises his assignment as though he's playing cover 2.

WEAK CORNER: Plays cover 1. Inside/outside technique is dependent upon field position and the distance of the split end's split. Disguises his assignment as though he's playing cover 2.

STUNT #76

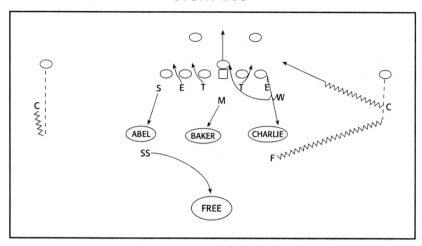

STUNT DESCRIPTION: This pro 4-3 **fire zone blitz** sends Whip and features a weakside cornerback blitz.

SECONDARY COVERAGE: Cover 1 disguised as cover 2. Mike, Stud, and the weak end drop into coverage, and the strong safety is free.

STRONG SAFETY: Lines up as though he's playing cover 2. During cadence, moves toward the deep middle. Provides alley support versus run and plays centerfield versus pass.

STUD: Plays 9 technique versus run. Drops **Abel** versus pass.

STRONG END: Slants into and secures the C gap versus run and contains the quarterback.

STRONG TACKLE: Cheats to a 2 technique and slants into the B gap.

MIKE: Pursues weakside and strongside run from an inside-out position. Drops **Baker** versus pass.

WEAK TACKLE: Slants into the B gap.

WEAK END: Plays 5 technique versus run. Drops **Charlie** versus pass.

WHIP: Creeps inside during cadence and stunts through the weakside A gap.

FREE SAFETY: Lines up as though he's playing cover 2. During cadence, moves to a position that enables him to cover the split end.

STRONG CORNER: Plays cover 1. Inside/outside technique is dependent upon field position and the distance of the flanker's split. Disguises his assignment as though he's playing cover 2.

WEAK CORNER: Creeps inside during cadence and blitzes from the edge. Contains the quarterback and weakside run. Chases strongside run.

STUNT #77

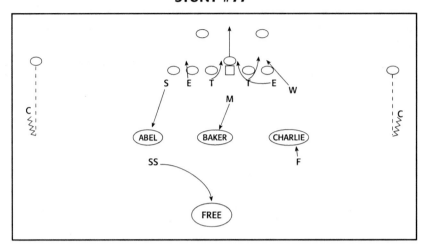

STUNT DESCRIPTION: This pro 4-3 **fire zone blitz** sends Whip and provides the defense with a weakside line twist.

SECONDARY COVERAGE: Cover 1 disguised as cover 2. The free safety, Mike, and Stud drop into coverage, and the strong safety plays centerfield.

STRONG SAFETY: Lines up as though he's playing cover 2. Contains strongside run and provides alley support versus weakside run. Plays centerfield versus pass.

STUD: Plays 9 technique versus run. Drops **Abel** versus pass.

STRONG END: Plays 5 technique versus run. Contains the quarterback versus pass.

STRONG TACKLE: Slants into the A gap.

MIKE: Secures the B gap versus strongside run and pursues weakside run from an inside-out position. Drops **Baker** versus pass.

WEAK TACKLE: Cheats to a 2 technique and slants into the B gap.

WEAK END: Loops behind the tackle into the weakside A gap.

WHIP: Rushes through the near shoulder of the offensive tackle. Secures the C gap versus run and contains the quarterback.

FREE SAFETY: Lines up as though he's playing cover 2. Contains weakside run and provides alley support versus strongside run. Drops **Charlie** versus pass.

STRONG CORNER: Plays cover 1. Inside/outside technique is dependent upon field position and the distance of the flanker's split. Disguises his assignment as though he's playing cover 2.

WEAK CORNER: Plays cover 1. Inside/outside technique is dependent upon field position and the distance of the split end's split. Disguises his assignment as though he's playing cover 2.

STUNT #78

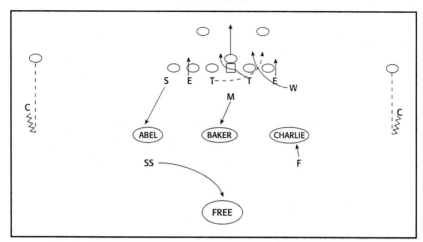

STUNT DESCRIPTION: This pro 4-3 **fire zone blitz** sends Whip and provides the defense with a delayed weakside twin stunt.

SECONDARY COVERAGE: Cover 1 disguised as cover 2. The free safety, Mike, and Stud drop into coverage, and the strong safety plays centerfield.

STRONG SAFETY: Lines up as though he's playing cover 2. Contains strongside run and provides alley support versus weakside run. Plays centerfield versus pass.

STUD: Plays 9 technique versus run. Drops **Abel** versus pass.

STRONG END: Plays 5 technique versus run. Contains the quarterback versus pass.

STRONG TACKLE: Plays 1 technique versus run. If he reads pass, he runs a delay line twist through the weakside B gap.

MIKE: Secures the B gap versus strongside run and pursues weakside run from an inside-out position. Drops **Baker** versus pass.

WEAK TACKLE: Plays 1 technique versus run. Attacks the center and works into the strongside A gap if he reads pass.

WEAK END: Plays 5 technique versus run. Contains the quarterback versus pass.

WHIP: Blitzes through the B gap at the snap of the ball.

FREE SAFETY: Lines up as though he's playing cover 2. Contains weakside run and provides alley support versus strongside run. Drops **Charlie** versus pass.

STRONG CORNER: Plays cover 1. Inside/outside technique is dependent upon field position and the distance of the flanker's split. Disguises his assignment as though he's playing cover 2.

WEAK CORNER: Plays cover 1. Inside/outside technique is dependent upon field position and the distance of the split end's split. Disguises his assignment as though he's playing cover 2.

STUNT #79

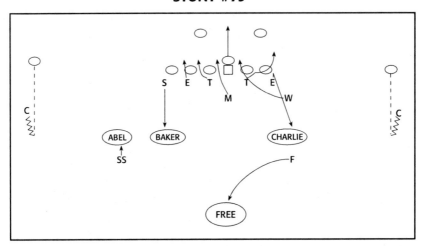

STUNT DESCRIPTION: This pro 4-3 **fire zone blitz** provides the defense with good inside pressure.

SECONDARY COVERAGE: Cover 1 disguised as cover 2. The strong safety, Stud and the weak end drop into coverage, and the free safety plays centerfield.

STRONG SAFETY: Lines up as though he's playing cover 2. Helps contain strongside run and provides alley support versus weakside run. Drops **Abel** versus pass.

STUD: Plays 9 technique versus run. Drops **Baker** versus pass.

STRONG END: Plays 5 technique versus run. Contains the quarterback versus pass.

STRONG TACKLE: Cheats to a 2 technique and slants to and secures the B gap.

MIKE: Blitzes through the strongside A gap.

WEAK TACKLE: Cheats to a 2 technique and slants to and secures the B gap versus run. Contain rushes versus pass.

WEAK END: Plays 5 technique versus run. Drops **Charlie** versus pass.

WHIP: Blitzes through the weakside A gap.

FREE SAFETY: Lines up as though he's playing cover 2. Helps contain weakside run and provides alley support versus strongside run. Drops to centerfield versus pass.

STRONG CORNER: Plays cover 1. Inside/outside technique is dependent upon field position and the distance of the flanker's split. Disguises his assignment as though he's playing cover 2.

WEAK CORNER: Plays cover 1. Inside/outside technique is dependent upon field position and the distance of the split end's split. Disguises his assignment as though he's playing cover 2.

STUNT #80

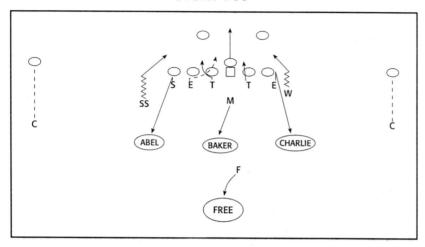

STUNT DESCRIPTION: This pro 4-3 **fire zone blitz** provides the defense with excellent outside pressure and a strongside twin stunt through the B gap.

SECONDARY COVERAGE: Cover 1 disguised as cover 3. Stud, Mike, and the weak end drop into coverage, and the free safety plays centerfield.

STRONG SAFETY: Lines up as though he's playing cover 3 sky. Creeps toward the line during cadence and rushes from the edge. Contains the quarterback and strongside run. Chases weakside run.

STUD: Plays 9 technique versus run. Drops **Abel** versus pass.

STRONG END: Plays 5 technique versus run. Delay stunts through the B gap versus pass.

STRONG TACKLE: Cheats to a 2 technique and secures the B gap versus run. Versus pass, rushes hard through the B gap.

MIKE: Controls the strongside A gap and the weakside B gap versus run. Drops **Baker** versus pass.

WEAK TACKLE: Plays 1 technique.

WEAK END: Plays 5 technique versus run. Drops **Charlie** versus pass.

WHIP: Rushes from the edge. Contains the quarterback and weakside run. Chases strongside run.

FREE SAFETY: Lines up as though he's playing cover 3. Provides alley support versus run. Plays centerfield versus pass.

STRONG CORNER: Plays cover 1. Inside/outside technique is dependent upon field position and the distance of the flanker's split.

WEAK CORNER: Plays cover 1. Inside/outside technique is dependent upon field position and the distance of the split end's split.

STUNT #81

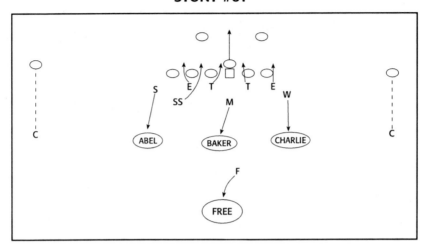

STUNT DESCRIPTION: This pro 4-3 **fire zone blitz** provides the defense with a strong safety blitz.

SECONDARY COVERAGE: Cover 1. Stud, Mike, and Whip drop into coverage, and the free safety plays centerfield.

STRONG SAFETY: Lines up four yards deep on the inside shoulder of the tight end. Blitzes through the B gap.

STUD: Plays 8 technique versus run. Drops **Abel** versus pass.

STRONG END: Stunts into the C gap.

STRONG TACKLE: Stunts into the A gap.

MIKE: Plugs the B gap versus weakside run and pursues strongside run from an inside-out position. Drops **Baker** versus pass.

WEAK TACKLE: Plays 1 technique.

WEAK END: Plays 5 technique versus run. Contains the quarterback versus pass.

WHIP: Plays 9 technique versus run. Drops **Charlie** versus pass.

FREE SAFETY: Lines up as though he's playing cover 3. Provides alley support versus run. Plays centerfield versus pass.

STRONG CORNER: Plays cover 1. Inside/outside technique is dependent upon field position and the distance of the flanker's split.

WEAK CORNER: Plays cover 1. Inside/outside technique is dependent upon field position and the distance of the split end's split.

STUNT #82

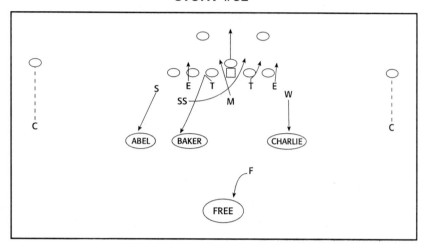

STUNT DESCRIPTION: This pro 4-3 **fire zone blitz** provides the defense with excellent inside pressure via a strong safety blitz.

SECONDARY COVERAGE: Cover 1. Stud, the strong tackle, and Whip drop into coverage, and the free safety plays centerfield.

STRONG SAFETY: Lines up four yards deep on the inside shoulder of the tight end. Blitzes through the weakside A gap.

STUD: Plays 8 technique versus run. Drops **Abel** versus pass.

STRONG END: Plays 5 technique versus run. Contains the quarterback versus pass.

STRONG TACKLE: Cheats to a 2 technique. Slants to and secures the B gap. Drops **Baker** versus pass.

MIKE: Blitzes through the strongside A gap.

WEAK TACKLE: Cheats to a 2 technique and secures the B gap versus run. Rushes through the B gap versus pass.

WEAK END: Plays 5 technique versus run. Contains the quarterback versus pass.

WHIP: Plays 9 technique versus run. Drops **Charlie** versus pass.

FREE SAFETY: Lines up as though he's playing cover 3. Provides alley support versus run. Plays centerfield versus pass.

STRONG CORNER: Plays cover 1. Inside/outside technique is dependent upon field position and the distance of the flanker's split.

WEAK CORNER: Plays cover 1. Inside/outside technique is dependent upon field position and the distance of the split end's split.

STUNT #83

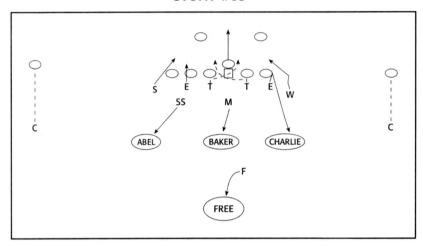

STUNT DESCRIPTION: This pro 4-3 **fire zone blitz** provides the defense with excellent outside pressure and a delayed line twist versus pass.

SECONDARY COVERAGE: Cover 1. The strong safety, Mike, and the weak end drop into coverage, and the free safety plays centerfield.

STRONG SAFETY: Lines up four yards deep on the inside shoulder of the tight end. Versus strongside run, scrapes outside and helps contain. Pursues weakside run from an inside-out position. Drops **Abel** versus pass.

STUD: Lines up in an 8 technique and rushes from the edge. Contains the quarterback and strongside run. Chases weakside run.

STRONG END: Plays 5 technique.

STRONG TACKLE: Plays 1 technique versus run. Versus pass, attacks the center and works into the weakside A gap.

MIKE: Secures both B gaps versus run. Drops **Baker** versus pass.

WEAK TACKLE: Plays 1 technique versus run. Versus pass, loops behind the left tackle into the strongside A gap.

WEAK END: Plays 5 technique versus run. Versus pass, drops **Charlie**.

WHIP: Rushes the edge. Contains the quarterback and weakside run. Chases strongside run.

FREE SAFETY: Lines up as though he's playing cover 3. Provides alley support versus run. Plays centerfield versus pass.

STRONG CORNER: Plays cover 1. Inside/outside technique is dependent upon field position and the distance of the flanker's split.

WEAK CORNER: Plays cover 1. Inside/outside technique is dependent upon field position and the distance of the split end's split.

STUNT #84

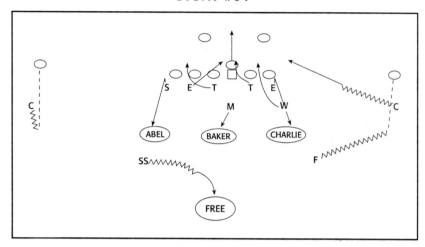

STUNT DESCRIPTION: This pro 4-3 **fire zone blitz** features a weakside cornerback blitz.

SECONDARY COVERAGE: Cover 1 disguised as cover 2. Mike, Stud, and the weak end drop into coverage, and the strong safety is free.

STRONG SAFETY: Lines up as though he's playing cover 2. During cadence, moves toward the deep middle. Provides alley support versus run and plays centerfield versus pass.

STUD: Plays 9 technique versus run. Drops **Abel** versus pass.

STRONG END: Slants to the near shoulder of the offensive guard and secures the B gap.

STRONG TACKLE: Cheats to a 2 technique and loops across the face of the offensive tackle. Controls the C gap and contains the quarterback.

MIKE: Secures the A gap versus strongside run. Pursues weakside run from an inside-out position. Drops **Baker** versus pass.

WEAK TACKLE: Attacks the near shoulder of the center and secures the weakside A gap.

WEAK END: Plays 5 technique versus run. Drops **Charlie** versus pass.

WHIP: Blitzes through the weakside B gap.

FREE SAFETY: Lines up as though he's playing cover 2. During cadence, moves to a position that enables him to cover the split end.

STRONG CORNER: Plays cover 1. Inside/outside technique is dependent upon field position and the distance of the flanker's split. Disguises his assignment as though he's playing cover 2.

WEAK CORNER: Creeps inside during cadence and blitzes from the edge. Contains the quarterback and weakside run. Chases strongside run.

STUNT #85

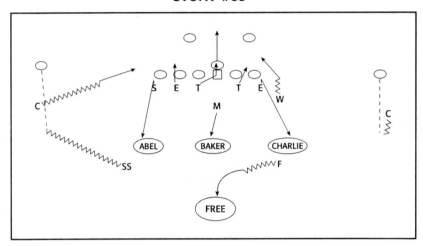

STUNT DESCRIPTION: This pro 4-3 **fire zone blitz** features a strongside cornerback blitz.

SECONDARY COVERAGE: Cover 1 disguised as cover 2. Mike, Stud, and the weak end drop into coverage, and the free safety plays centerfield.

STRONG SAFETY: Lines up as though he's playing cover 2. During cadence, moves to a position that enables him to cover the flanker.

STUD: Plays 9 technique versus run. Drops **Abel** versus pass.

STRONG END: Plays 5 technique.

STRONG TACKLE: Slants into the near shoulder of the center and controls the strongside A gap.

MIKE: Plugs the B gap versus strongside run and secures the A gap versus weakside run. Drops **Baker** versus pass.

WEAK TACKLE: Cheats to a 2 technique and slants into the B gap.

WEAK END: Plays 5 technique versus run. Drops **Charlie** versus pass.

WHIP: Rushes from the edge. Contains the quarterback and weakside run. Chases strongside run.

FREE SAFETY: Lines up as though he's playing cover 2. During cadence, moves toward the deep middle. Provides alley support versus run and plays centerfield versus pass.

STRONG CORNER: Creeps inside during cadence and blitzes from the edge. Contains the quarterback and strongside run. Chases weakside run.

WEAK CORNER: Plays cover 1. Inside/outside technique is dependent upon field position and the distance of the split end's split. Disguises his assignment as though he's playing cover 2.

CHAPTER 8

BEAR 46 FIRE ZONE BLITZES

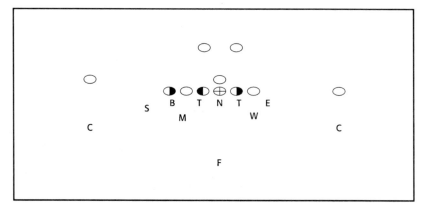

Figure 8-1

Stud—Outside linebacker aligned on the tight-end side in an 8 technique.

Buck—Outside linebacker aligned on the tight-end side in a 7 technique.

Mike—Inside linebacker aligned on the tight-end side (often a strong-safety type).

Strong tackle—3 technique aligned on the tight-end side.

Nose—0 technique.

Weak tackle—3 technique aligned on the split-end side.

Whip—Weakside linebacker.

Weak end—7 technique aligned on the split-end side.

Strong cornerback—Cornerback aligned opposite the flanker.

Weak cornerback—Cornerback aligned opposite the split end.

Free safety—Defensive back aligned in centerfield.

STUNT #86

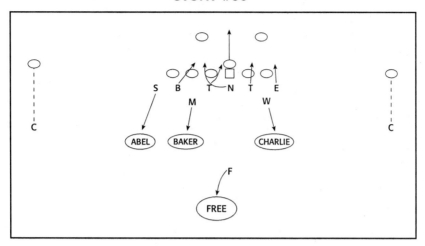

STUNT DESCRIPTION: This Bear 46 **fire zone blitz** sends Buck and provides the defense with a strongside line twist.

SECONDARY COVERAGE: Cover 1. Stud, Mike, and Whip drop into coverage, and the free safety plays centerfield.

STUD: Plays 8 technique versus run. Drops **Abel** versus pass.

BUCK: Slants into the near shoulder of the offensive tackle and secures the C gap. Contains the quarterback versus pass.

MIKE: Plays base technique versus run. Drops **Baker** versus pass.

STRONG TACKLE: Slants across the face of the offensive guard into the A gap.

NOSE: Loops behind the slanting tackle into the strongside B gap.

WEAK TACKLE: Plays 3 technique.

WEAK END: Plays 7 technique versus run. Contains the quarterback versus pass.

WHIP: Plays base technique versus run. Drops **Charlie** versus pass.

FREE SAFETY: Lines up as though he's playing cover 3. Provides alley support versus run. Plays centerfield versus pass.

STRONG CORNER: Plays cover 1. Inside/outside technique is dependent upon field position and the distance of the flanker's split.

WEAK CORNER: Plays cover 1. Inside/outside technique is dependent upon field position and the distance of the split end's split.

STUNT #87

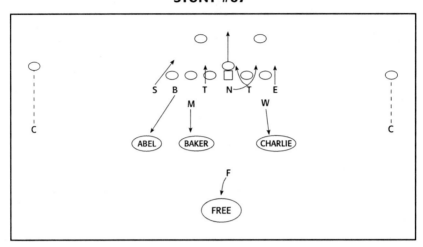

STUNT DESCRIPTION: This Bear 46 **fire zone blitz** sends Stud and provides the defense with a weakside line twist.

SECONDARY COVERAGE: Cover 1. Buck, Mike, and Whip drop into coverage, and the free safety plays centerfield.

STUD: Rushes from the edge. Contains the quarterback and strongside run. Chases weakside run.

BUCK: Plays 7 technique versus run. Drops **Abel** versus pass.

MIKE: Plays base technique versus run. Drops **Baker** versus pass.

STRONG TACKLE: Plays 3 technique.

NOSE: Loops behind the slanting tackle into the weakside B gap.

WEAK TACKLE: Slants across the face of the offensive guard into the A gap.

WEAK END: Plays 7 technique versus run. Contains the quarterback versus pass.

WHIP: Plays base technique versus run. Drops **Charlie** versus pass.

FREE SAFETY: Lines up as though he's playing cover 3. Provides alley support versus run. Plays centerfield versus pass.

STRONG CORNER: Plays cover 1. Inside/outside technique is dependent upon field position and the distance of the flanker's split.

WEAK CORNER: Plays cover 1. Inside/outside technique is dependent upon field position and the distance of the split end's split.

STUNT #88

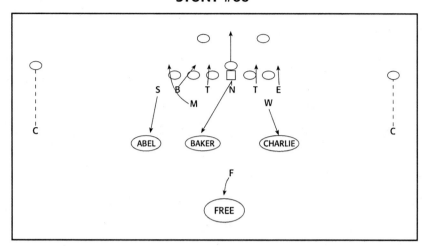

STUNT DESCRIPTION: This Bear 46 **fire zone blitz** sends both Buck and Mike.

SECONDARY COVERAGE: Cover 1. Stud, nose, and Whip drop into coverage, and the free safety plays centerfield.

STUD: Plays 8 technique versus run. Drops **Abel** versus pass.

BUCK: Attacks the near shoulder of the offensive tackle and secures the C gap.

MIKE: Blitzes through the outside shoulder of the tight end. Secures the D gap and contains the quarterback.

STRONG TACKLE: Plays 3 technique.

NOSE: Plays 0 technique versus run. Drops **Baker** versus pass.

WEAK TACKLE: Plays 3 technique.

WEAK END: Plays 7 technique versus run. Contains the quarterback versus pass.

WHIP: Plays base technique versus run. Drops **Charlie** versus pass.

FREE SAFETY: Lines up as though he's playing cover 3. Provides alley support versus run. Plays centerfield versus pass.

STRONG CORNER: Plays cover 1. Inside/outside technique is dependent upon field position and the distance of the flanker's split.

WEAK CORNER: Plays cover 1. Inside/outside technique is dependent upon field position and the distance of the split end's split.

STUNT #89

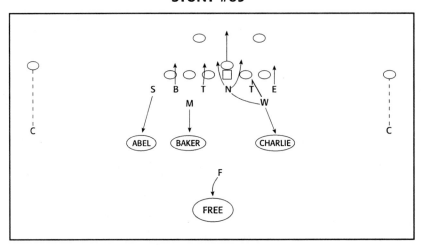

STUNT DESCRIPTION: This Bear 46 **fire zone blitz** sends both Whip and Buck.

SECONDARY COVERAGE: Cover 1. Stud, Mike, and the weak tackle drop into coverage, and the free safety plays centerfield.

STUD: Plays 8 technique versus run. Drops **Abel** versus pass.

BUCK: Plays 7 technique versus run. Contains the quarterback versus pass.

MIKE: Plays base technique versus run. Drops **Baker** versus pass.

STRONG TACKLE: Plays 3 technique.

NOSE: Stunts into the weakside A gap.

WEAK TACKLE: Plays 3 technique versus run. Drops **Charlie** versus pass.

WEAK END: Plays 7 technique versus run. Contains the quarterback versus pass.

WHIP: Blitzes through the strongside A gap.

FREE SAFETY: Lines up as though he's playing cover 3. Provides alley support versus run. Plays centerfield versus pass.

STRONG CORNER: Plays cover 1. Inside/outside technique is dependent upon field position and the distance of the flanker's split.

WEAK CORNER: Plays cover 1. Inside/outside technique is dependent upon field position and the distance of the split end's split.

STUNT #90

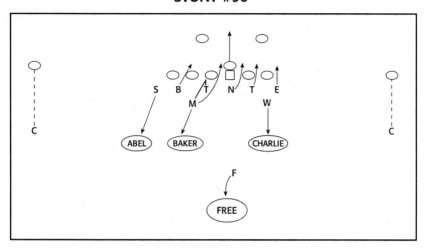

STUNT DESCRIPTION: This Bear 46 **fire zone blitz** sends Mike and Buck.

SECONDARY COVERAGE: Cover 1. Stud, Whip, and the strong tackle drop into coverage, and the free safety plays centerfield.

STUD: Plays 8 technique versus run. Drops **Abel** versus pass.

BUCK: Slants to the near shoulder of the offensive tackle. Secures the C gap and contains the quarterback.

MIKE: Blitzes through the strongside A gap.

STRONG TACKLE: Plays 3 technique versus run. Drops **Baker** versus pass.

NOSE: Stunts into the weakside A gap.

WEAK TACKLE: Plays 3 technique.

WEAK END: Plays 7 technique versus run. Contains the quarterback versus pass.

WHIP: Plays base technique versus run. Drops **Charlie** versus pass.

FREE SAFETY: Lines up as though he's playing cover 3. Provides alley support versus run. Plays centerfield versus pass.

STRONG CORNER: Plays cover 1. Inside/outside technique is dependent upon field position and the distance of the flanker's split.

WEAK CORNER: Plays cover 1. Inside/outside technique is dependent upon field position and the distance of the split end's split.

STUNT #91

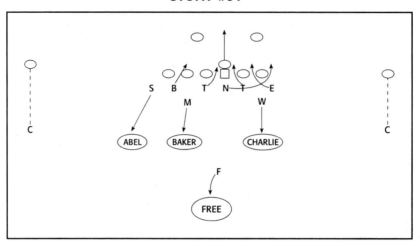

STUNT DESCRIPTION: This Bear 46 **fire zone blitz** sends Buck and provides the defense with a weakside line twist.

SECONDARY COVERAGE: Cover 1. Stud, Mike, and Whip drop into coverage, and the free safety plays centerfield.

STUD: Plays 8 technique versus run. Drops **Abel** versus pass.

BUCK: Slants to the near shoulder of the offensive tackle and controls the C gap. Contains the quarterback versus pass.

MIKE: Plays base technique versus run. Drops **Baker** versus pass.

STRONG TACKLE: Slants across the offensive guard's face into the strongside A gap.

NOSE: Loops across the face of the weakside offensive tackle. Secures the C gap and contains the quarterback.

WEAK TACKLE: Slants across the face of the offensive guard into the weakside A gap.

WEAK END: Slants across the offensive tackle's face into the B gap.

WHIP: Plays base technique versus run. Drops **Charlie** versus pass.

FREE SAFETY: Lines up as though he's playing cover 3. Provides alley support versus run. Plays centerfield versus pass.

STRONG CORNER: Plays cover 1. Inside/outside technique is dependent upon field position and the distance of the flanker's split.

WEAK CORNER: Plays cover 1. Inside/outside technique is dependent upon field position and the distance of the split end's split.

STUNT #92

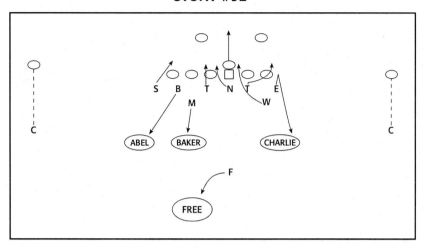

STUNT DESCRIPTION: This Bear 46 **fire zone blitz** sends both Stud and Whip.

SECONDARY COVERAGE: Cover 1. The weak end, Buck and Mike drop into coverage, and the free safety plays centerfield.

STUD: Rushes from the edge. Contains the quarterback and strongside run. Chases weakside run.

BUCK: Plays 7 technique versus run. Drops **Abel** versus pass.

MIKE: Plays base technique versus run. Drops **Baker** versus pass.

STRONG TACKLE: Plays 3 technique.

NOSE: Slants into the strongside A gap.

WEAK TACKLE: Plays 3 technique versus run. Contain rushes versus pass.

WEAK END: Plays 7 technique versus run. Drops **Charlie** versus pass.

WHIP: Blitzes through the weakside A gap.

FREE SAFETY: Lines up as though he's playing cover 3. Provides alley support versus run. Plays centerfield versus pass.

STRONG CORNER: Plays cover 1. Inside/outside technique is dependent upon field position and the distance of the flanker's split.

WEAK CORNER: Plays cover 1. Inside/outside technique is dependent upon field position and the distance of the split end's split.

STUNT #93

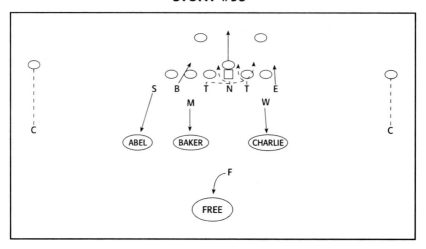

STUNT DESCRIPTION: This Bear 46 **fire zone blitz** sends Buck and provides the defense with a delayed, weakside line twist versus pass.

SECONDARY COVERAGE: Cover 1. Stud, Mike, and Whip drop into coverage, and the free safety plays centerfield.

STUD: Plays 8 technique versus run. Drops **Abel** versus pass.

BUCK: Slants to the near shoulder of the offensive tackle and controls the C gap. Contains the quarterback versus pass.

MIKE: Plays base technique versus run. Drops **Baker** versus pass.

STRONG TACKLE: Plays 3 technique versus run. Versus pass, loops into the weakside B gap.

NOSE: Plays 0 technique versus run. Versus pass, slants through the strongside A gap.

WEAK TACKLE: Plays 3 technique versus run. Versus pass, slants through the weakside A gap.

WEAK END: Plays 7 technique versus run. Contains the quarterback versus pass.

WHIP: Plays base technique versus run. Drops **Charlie** versus pass.

FREE SAFETY: Lines up as though he's playing cover 3. Provides alley support versus run. Plays centerfield versus pass.

STRONG CORNER: Plays cover 1. Inside/outside technique is dependent upon field position and the distance of the flanker's split.

WEAK CORNER: Plays cover 1. Inside/outside technique is dependent upon field position and the distance of the split end's split.

STUNT #94

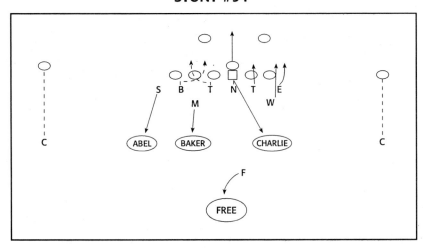

STUNT DESCRIPTION: This Bear 46 **fire zone blitz** sends Whip and provides the defense with a strongside line twist.

SECONDARY COVERAGE: Cover 1. Stud, Mike, and nose drop into coverage, and the free safety plays centerfield.

STUD: Plays 8 technique versus run. Drops **Abel** versus pass.

BUCK: Plays 7 technique versus run. Versus pass, loops behind the defensive tackle into the B gap.

MIKE: Plays base technique versus run. Drops **Baker** versus pass.

STRONG TACKLE: Plays 3 technique versus run. Contain rushes versus pass.

NOSE: Plays 0 technique versus run. Drops **Charlie** versus pass.

WEAK TACKLE: Plays 3 technique.

WEAK END: Slants outside. Contains the quarterback and weakside run. Chases strongside run.

WHIP: Blitzes through the outside shoulder of the offensive tackle and secures the C gap.

FREE SAFETY: Lines up as though he's playing cover 3. Provides alley support versus run. Plays centerfield versus pass.

STRONG CORNER: Plays cover 1. Inside/outside technique is dependent upon field position and the distance of the flanker's split.

WEAK CORNER: Plays cover 1. Inside/outside technique is dependent upon field position and the distance of the split end's split.

STUNT #95

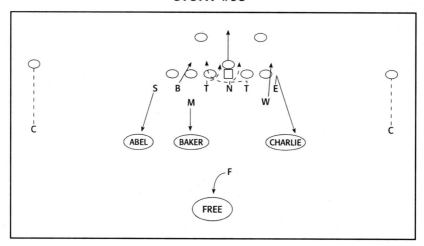

STUNT DESCRIPTION: This Bear 46 **fire zone blitz** sends Whip and provides the defense with a delayed strongside line twist versus pass.

SECONDARY COVERAGE: Cover 1. Stud, Mike, and the weak end drop into coverage, and the free safety plays centerfield.

STUD: Plays 8 technique versus run. Drops **Abel** versus pass.

BUCK: Attacks the near shoulder of the offensive tackle. Secures the C gap and contains the quarterback.

MIKE: Plays base technique versus run. Drops **Baker** versus pass.

STRONG TACKLE: Plays 3 technique versus run. Slants into the A gap versus pass.

NOSE: Plays 0 technique versus run. Slants into the weakside A gap versus pass.

WEAK TACKLE: Plays 3 technique versus run. Loops into the strongside B gap versus pass.

WEAK END: Plays 7 technique versus run. Drops **Charlie** versus pass.

WHIP: Blitzes through the outside shoulder of the offensive tackle and secures the C gap.

FREE SAFETY: Lines up as though he's playing cover 3. Provides alley support versus run. Plays centerfield versus pass.

STRONG CORNER: Plays cover 1. Inside/outside technique is dependent upon field position and the distance of the flanker's split.

WEAK CORNER: Plays cover 1. Inside/outside technique is dependent upon field position and the distance of the split end's split.

STUNT #96

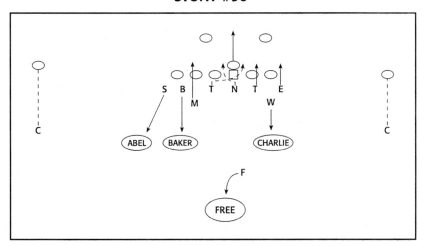

STUNT DESCRIPTION: This Bear 46 **fire zone blitz** sends Mike and provides the defense with a delayed line twist.

SECONDARY COVERAGE: Cover 1. Stud, Buck, and Whip drop into coverage, and the free safety plays centerfield.

STUD: Plays 8 technique versus run. Drops **Abel** versus pass.

BUCK: Plays 7 technique versus run. Drops **Baker** versus pass.

MIKE: Blitzes through the outside shoulder of the offensive tackle. Secures the C gap and contains the quarterback.

STRONG TACKLE: Plays 3 technique versus run. Loops into the weakside A gap versus pass.

NOSE: Plays 0 technique versus run. Slants into the strongside A gap versus pass.

WEAK TACKLE: Plays 3 technique.

WEAK END: Plays 7 technique versus run. Contains the quarterback versus pass.

WHIP: Plays base technique versus run. Drops **Charlie** versus pass.

FREE SAFETY: Lines up as though he's playing cover 3. Provides alley support versus run. Plays centerfield versus pass.

STRONG CORNER: Plays cover 1. Inside/outside technique is dependent upon field position and the distance of the flanker's split.

WEAK CORNER: Plays cover 1. Inside/outside technique is dependent upon field position and the distance of the split end's split.

STUNT #97

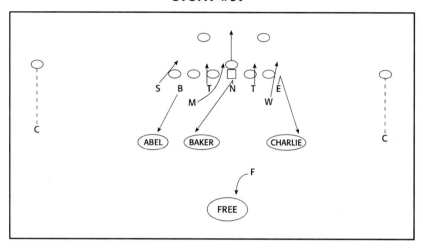

STUNT DESCRIPTION: This Bear 46 **fire zone blitz** sends Stud, Mike, and Whip.

SECONDARY COVERAGE: Cover 1. Buck, nose and the weak end drop into coverage, and the free safety plays centerfield.

STUD: Rushes from the edge. Contains the quarterback and strongside run. Chases weakside run.

BUCK: Plays 7 technique versus run. Drops **Abel** versus pass.

MIKE: Blitzes through the strongside A gap.

STRONG TACKLE: Plays 3 technique.

NOSE: Plays 0 technique versus run. Drops **Baker** versus pass.

WEAK TACKLE: Plays 3 technique.

WEAK END: Plays 7 technique versus run. Drops **Charlie** versus pass.

WHIP: Blitzes through the outside shoulder of the offensive tackle and secures the C gap.

FREE SAFETY: Lines up as though he's playing cover 3. Provides alley support versus run. Plays centerfield versus pass.

STRONG CORNER: Plays cover 1. Inside/outside technique is dependent upon field position and the distance of the flanker's split.

WEAK CORNER: Plays cover 1. Inside/outside technique is dependent upon field position and the distance of the split end's split.

STUNT #98

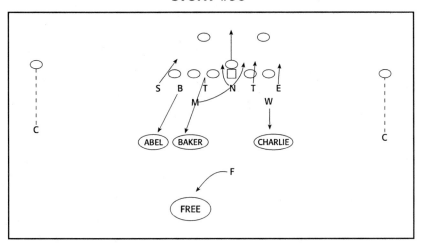

STUNT DESCRIPTION: This bear 46 **fire zone blitz** sends Mike and Stud.

SECONDARY COVERAGE: Cover 1. Buck, the strong tackle, and Whip drop into coverage, and the free safety plays centerfield.

STUD: Rushes from the edge. Contains the quarterback and strongside run. Chases weakside run.

BUCK: Plays 7 technique versus run. Drops **Abel** versus pass.

MIKE: Blitzes through the weakside A gap.

STRONG TACKLE: Plays 3 technique versus run. Drops **Baker** versus pass.

NOSE: Slants into the strongside A gap.

WEAK TACKLE: Plays 3 technique.

WEAK END: Plays 7 technique versus run. Contains the quarterback versus pass.

WHIP: Plays base technique versus run. Drops **Charlie** versus pass.

FREE SAFETY: Lines up as though he's playing cover 3. Provides alley support versus run. Plays centerfield versus pass.

STRONG CORNER: Plays cover 1. Inside/outside technique is dependent upon field position and the distance of the flanker's split.

WEAK CORNER: Plays cover 1. Inside/outside technique is dependent upon field position and the distance of the split end's split.

STUNT #99

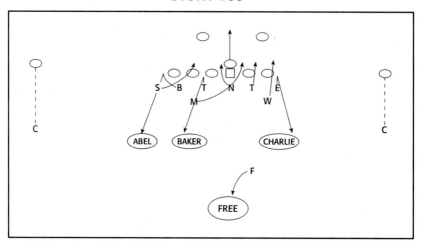

STUNT DESCRIPTION: This Bear 46 **fire zone blitz** sends Stud, Mike, and Whip.

SECONDARY COVERAGE: Cover 1. Buck, the strong tackle, and weak end drop into coverage, and the free safety plays centerfield.

STUD: Blitzes through the near shoulder of the offensive tackle. Secures the C gap and contains the quarterback.

BUCK: Slants across the face of the tight end into the D gap. Contains strongside run, chases weakside run, and drops **Abel** versus pass.

MIKE: Blitzes through the weakside A gap.

STRONG TACKLE: Plays 3 technique versus run. Drops **Baker** versus pass.

NOSE: Slants into the strongside A gap.

WEAK TACKLE: Plays 3 technique.

WEAK END: Plays 7 technique versus run. Drops **Charlie** versus pass.

WHIP: Blitzes through the outside shoulder of the offensive tackle. Secures the C gap and contains the quarterback.

FREE SAFETY: Lines up as though he's playing cover 3. Provides alley support versus run. Plays centerfield versus pass.

STRONG CORNER: Plays cover 1. Inside/outside technique is dependent upon field position and the distance of the flanker's split.

WEAK CORNER: Plays cover 1. Inside/outside technique is dependent upon field position and the distance of the split end's split.

STUNT #100

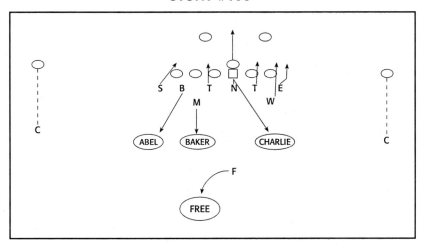

STUNT DESCRIPTION: This Bear 46 **fire zone blitz** sends Whip and Stud.

SECONDARY COVERAGE: Cover 1. Buck, nose, and Mike drop into coverage, and the free safety plays centerfield.

STUD: Rushes from the edge. Contains the quarterback and strongside run. Chases weakside run.

BUCK: Plays 7 technique versus run. Drops **Abel** versus pass.

MIKE: Plays base technique versus run. Drops **Baker** versus pass.

STRONG TACKLE: Plays 3 technique.

NOSE: Plays 0 technique versus run. Drops **Charlie** versus pass.

WEAK TACKLE: Plays 3 technique.

WEAK END: Slants outside. Contains the quarterback and weakside run. Chases strongside run.

WHIP: Blitzes through the outside shoulder of the offensive tackle and secures the C gap.

FREE SAFETY: Lines up as though he's playing cover 3. Provides alley support versus run. Plays centerfield versus pass.

STRONG CORNER: Plays cover 1. Inside/outside technique is dependent upon field position and the distance of the flanker's split.

WEAK CORNER: Plays cover 1. Inside/outside technique is dependent upon field position and the distance of the split end's split.

STUNT #101

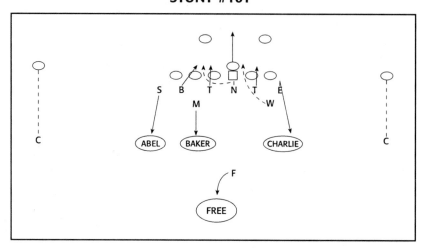

STUNT DESCRIPTION: This bear 46 **fire zone blitz** provides the defense with a delayed blitz by Whip and a delayed strongside twin stunt.

SECONDARY COVERAGE: Cover 1. Stud, Mike, and the weak end drop into coverage, and the free safety plays centerfield.

STUD: Plays 8 technique versus run. Drops **Abel** versus pass.

BUCK: Attacks the near shoulder of the offensive tackle. Secures the C gap and contains the quarterback.

MIKE: Plays base technique versus run. Drops **Baker** versus pass.

STRONG TACKLE: Plays 3 technique.

NOSE: Plays 0 technique versus run. Loops into the strongside B gap (twin stunt) versus pass.

WEAK TACKLE: Plays 3 technique.

WEAK END: Plays 7 technique versus run. Drops **Charlie** versus pass.

WHIP: Plays base technique versus run. Delay blitzes through the weakside A gap versus pass.

FREE SAFETY: Lines up as though he's playing cover 3. Provides alley support versus run. Plays centerfield versus pass.

STRONG CORNER: Plays cover 1. Inside/outside technique is dependent upon field position and the distance of the flanker's split.

WEAK CORNER: Plays cover 1. Inside/outside technique is dependent upon field position and the distance of the split end's split.

CHAPTER 9

A FIRE ZONE BLITZ PHILOSOPHY OF DEFENSE

Fire zone blitz defenders are not counterpunchers. They don't react; they attack. They're a rowdy bunch. They've got an attitude, a bad attitude. They're the aggressors, the pursuers, the raiders, the invaders. To be a member of this elite group, a man must be a warrior. To be a warrior, he must be willing to sell out every single play, to play with reckless abandon, to hold nothing back. To be a warrior, a man must be mentally and physically tough. He must be totally unselfish; he must be disciplined. He must take it upon himself to personally take the ball away from the offense. The four underlying factors of the fire zone blitz philosophy are: to be multiple, to be different, to disguise, and to attack.

TO BE MULTIPLE

You want to present the offense with many different fronts and coverages. You want them to spend a lot of time trying to prepare for you. You want to burden them mentally. There is no *best* front or coverage versus a single offensive formation or tactic. Despite a defense's physical ability, it will eventually get picked apart by a good offense if it attempts to sit in a single defense all evening.

TO BE DIFFERENT

Geronimo didn't fight like the cavalry. His strategy and tactics kept them in a constant state of confusion; consequently, it took one-third of the United States Cavalry (5,000+ men) to force Geronimo and his band of 34 Chiricahua renegades to surrender. You want to fight like Geronimo. You want to be different, more creative, more intelligent, and better than any other defense in America.

TO DISGUISE

You want to force each of your opponents to have to deal with both a pre-snap and a post-snap read. You want to show one look before the ball is snapped and then do something entirely different after the snap. You want to stem and shift while the quarterback is calling signals. You never want to afford a physically superior opponent the luxury of "lining up, winding up, and kicking gluteus maximus." You want to keep your opponents on their heels. You want them constantly guessing about what you're going to do.

TO ATTACK

Attack the Quarterback: You must sack the quarterback, or force him to throw off balance. You must force him to make bad decisions and hurried throws. You want to intimidate the quarterback and extinguish his enthusiasm, poise, and confidence.

Attack the Receivers: You want to taunt and torment them, knock them around. You want to disrupt their timing by forcing them to run collision courses and then KO them should they ever be lucky enough to catch the ball.

Attack the Running Backs: You want to pursue relentlessly, to stalk and swarm ballcarriers like a pack of hungry wolves. You want to pillage their enthusiasm by constantly pounding and punishing them.

Attack the Offensive Linemen: You want to overload their minds with a multitude of fronts, stunts, and line twists. You want to complicate and confuse their blocking assignments, and to curb their aggression by creating havoc.

Attack Game Plans: You want to take away what your opponents do best and force them to do something that they don't want to do. You want to control the game and force them to play it by your rules.

Attack the Ball: It's your ball, not theirs! You must rip it, strip it, recover it, snatch it out of the air, and then score with it.

ABOUT THE AUTHOR

Leo Hand is the defensive coordinator at El Paso (TX) High School, a position he assumed in 2001. Prior to that, he held the same job at Irvin High School in El Paso, Texas. With over 33 years of experience as a teacher and coach, Hand has served in a variety of coaching positions in his career. At each stop, he has achieved a notable level of success.

A graduate of Emporia State University in Emporia, Kansas, Hand began his football coaching career in 1968 as the junior varsity coach at McQuaid Jesuit High School in Rochester, New York. After two seasons, he then accepted the job as the offensive line coach at Aquinas Institute (1970-'71). Next, he served as the head coach at Saint John Fisher College — a position he held for two years. He has also served on the gridiron staffs at APW (Parrish, NY) High School (head coach); Saint Anthony (Long Beach, CA) High School (head coach), Daniel Murphy (Los Angeles, CA) High School (head coach), Servite (Anaheim, CA) High School (head coach); Serra (Gardena, CA) High School (head coach); Long Beach (CA) City College (offensive line and linebackers); and Los Angeles (CA) Harbor College (offensive coordinator).

During the six-year period he spent coaching interscholastic teams in California, Hand's squads won 81 percent of their games in the highly competitive area of Southern California. At Serra High School, his teams compiled a 24-1 record, won a CIF championship, and were declared California State champions. On numerous occasions, he has helped rebuild several floundering gridiron teams into highly successful programs. For his efforts, he has been honored on numerous occasions with Coach-of-the-Year recognition.

A former Golden Gloves boxing champion, Hand is a prolific author, having written several football instructional books and numerous articles that have been published. He and his wife, Mary, have nine children and seven grandchildren.